ADVENTURES IN ALASKA WITH MY ANGEL JOE

LES BINGMAN

WESTBOW
PRESS®
A DIVISION OF THOMAS NELSON
& ZONDERVAN

WestBow Press books may be ordered through booksellers or by contacting:

WestBow Press
A Division of Thomas Nelson & Zondervan
1663 Liberty Drive
Bloomington, IN 47403
www.westbowpress.com
1 (866) 928-1240

ISBN: 978-1-9736-1038-0 (sc)
ISBN: 978-1-9736-1039-7 (hc)
ISBN: 978-1-9736-1037-3 (e)

Library of Congress Control Number: 2017918810

Print information available on the last page.

WestBow Press rev. date: 12/08/2017

CONTENTS

PREFACE

Adventures in Alaska with My Angel Joe tells the true story of a young man's near-death experiences growing up in bush Alaska. Raised in the company of some of the best bush pilots and commercial salmon fishermen in Bristol Bay, the young man tries to mimic the men he grew up idolizing. This proves harder than he imagined, and instead of becoming a bush pilot as he had dreamed, he repeatedly finds himself in potentially deadly situations involving airplanes and boats because of his naïveté. After experiencing subtle miracles firsthand, he begins to recognize feelings and signals that he believes could only come from his own personal guardian angel.

What are subtle miracles? Imagine a young boy running after a ball. The ball is rolling out into the street. As the boy reaches the curb, he trips and falls just as a fast-moving vehicle speeds by that would have hit the boy if he hadn't tripped and fallen. The same boy, years later, is learning to drive a stick shift and has perfected leaping off the line when the stoplight turns green. One day, he is waiting for the green light so he can show his friends how good he is at his newfound skill. A millisecond before the light turns green, his foot slips off the clutch, and with his right foot still on the brake, the vehicle stalls. The light turns green, and a large truck speeds by, running the red light.

After experiencing miracles like these repeatedly, the young boy in Alaska begins to realize that his guardian angel—who he eventually names Joe—never leaves his side. Most of us throughout our lives have near-death experiences, and often we credit our survival to luck, never giving credit to our guardian angels even though the Bible refers to them repeatedly.

The young Alaskan boy eventually realizes he is chasing an unrealistic dream and tries to alter his reckless behavior. Unfortunately, his daring ways are so embedded into his personality that despite his efforts to change, he continues to test his angel Joe's ability to protect him. Whether out on the ocean or up in the sky, Joe is always there, sitting quietly by and letting the young man live his life until a gentle whisper or a sign is needed to get him back on track. Joe will even appear as flesh and blood if that is what is required.

As you read this book, I hope you will reflect on subtle miracles that have happened in your life and, with God's help, start to realize that you are never truly alone.

Chapter 1

ASSIGNED AN ANGEL

Alaska is separated from the lower forty-eight by a considerable distance. The landscape is vast and rugged, with a climate to match. In the past, Alaska has been without formal government, presided over by the War Department, the US Treasury, and the US Navy. When Alaska was defined as a civil and judicial district, that allowed for a government, a code of law, and a federal court. None of this made any difference to the hardy group of individuals who were slowly trickling into Alaska because of the opportunities to hunt, fish, trap, and live off the land—and let's not forget the gold. These individuals occupied areas of Alaska that were very remote, with few doctors and little if any law enforcement.

Southwest Alaska is slightly larger than California and encompasses the immense area where I grew up. It includes the 6.4 million acres now known as Togiak National Wildlife Refuge and the 4.2 million acres of Wood-Tikchik State Park, along with many other parks and refuges. It also includes vast mountain ranges and large interior lakes.

The Bering Sea is a northern extension of the Pacific Ocean. It separates two continents and is bordered by Russia on the west.

The Aleutian Islands represent the southern border, and in the east Alaska enjoys a vigorous and productive ecosystem. Bristol Bay is a large body of water in the eastern Bering Sea north of the Alaska Peninsula. Bristol Bay supports the world's largest runs of wild sockeye salmon and returns of other species of Pacific salmon.

Nushagak Bay opens to Bristol Bay. Dillingham is on Nushagak Bay at the mouth of the Nushagak River, an inlet of Bristol Bay, an arm of the Bering Sea in the North Pacific, in Southwest Alaska. Nushagak was a trade center and settlement near the present-day site of Dillingham, at the northern end of Nushagak Bay in northern Bristol Bay. It was located near the confluence of the Wood and Nushagak Rivers. The Russians built a Russian Orthodox mission and a trading post at Nushagak Point in 1818, and the settlement was called Nushagak. Nushagak became a place where different Alaskan native groups from the Kuskokwim River, the Alaska Peninsula, and Cook Inlet came to trade or live.

In 1881, after the Alaska Purchase by the United States, the US Signal Corps built a weather station at Nushagak Point. The first salmon cannery in the Bristol Bay region was constructed in 1883 at Kanulik, just east of Nushagak Point. Several other canneries followed, two of which were at Nushagak Point.

The worldwide influenza pandemic of 1918 devastated the region in 1919, and this contributed to the depopulation of Nushagak. After the epidemic, a hospital and an orphanage were established in Kanakanak, across the river and six miles from the present-day city center of Dillingham. The mudflats at Nushagak Point were steadily growing, and by 1936, they were so extensive that it was no longer usable as a cannery site.

Present Day Nushagak Point

By the 1960s, Nushagak Point had become a popular location to fish from the beach using a fifty-fathom gill net anchored perpendicular to the shoreline. This method of fishing is called set netting. My mom stayed in a small cabin at Nushagak Point that my parents rented from an established fisherman, and she fished her own set net there. My dad fished out in the bay with his wooden double-ended powerboat. The boat had a small cabin located in the front with a separate enclosed driving station. The driving station was open in the back toward the fishing area. The boat had a gas engine close to the middle of the boat, with a shaft leading to a prop. Behind the prop was a rudder operated by cables and chains from the driving station.

In June of 1961, my mom left the state of Alaska just before I was born to be around her sister while giving birth. Shortly after my birth, she returned to Alaska, leaving me with my aunt for several months while she finished the commercial fishing season. Dillingham had around six hundred year-round residents at the time. It had a small Seventh Day Adventist church that my parents were members of. The church was located near the center of town. My parents were renting a small shack on the outskirts of Dillingham city center, about a mile from the airport.

By the time I arrived in Alaska, six months after my birth, airplanes were playing a major role in the everyday transportation needs of the villages, beaches, and structures that surrounded Dillingham. The brave men flying these airplanes had already earned the nickname "bush pilots." They were flying airplanes relative to that era. They navigated from village to village simply by knowing the area. They followed brush patterns, tree lines, and rivers like they were roads.

I grew up listening to the stories of heroic flights—tales of people being picked up in the middle of nowhere and taken to hospitals, or of mothers being transported to give birth at a hospital rather than at a remote location. The Kanakanak Hospital in Dillingham, specifically, was where people would come from hundreds of miles away to get medical attention. Anchorage, one of the largest cities by population in Alaska, was a place where you would be sent if your needs were beyond what could be provided at Kanakanak. Bush pilots were the only means of transportation to the hospital at Kanakanak—or if you were really in bad shape, to the hospital in Anchorage. I would listen to numerous stories of illnesses and accidents of all types, including accidental shootings that required transporting of the victim by a small plane to Anchorage, about 450 miles northeast of Dillingham.

I have been around airplanes as far back as I can remember. My mom used to tell a story about me when I was only four or five years old. My dad was working as a mechanic's assistant at my uncle's aircraft repair shop. My dad had finished working on a 1959 Cessna 150 airplane that had two seats side by side and an area behind the two seats that was large enough to accommodate a large dog. It was a tricycle-gear general aviation airplane that was designed for flight training, touring, and personal use. The plane was about twenty-three feet long with a thirty-three foot wingspan, and it was pulled along by a 100-horsepower engine.

After working on someone's airplane, my dad, still trying to build flight time, would take advantage of the opportunity to test-fly any aircraft he worked on. With the Cessna 150, he decided to bring my mom and me along as passengers. Apparently my dad was a good enough mechanic to have gotten the airplane running and up to about a thousand feet before the engine quit. The way my mom tells the story, as my dad was gliding down to make a landing at the airport, I was standing up in the back with my little hands folded and my eyes shut. I was explaining to God that I was too young to die—and apparently, he was listening because we landed without any problems. Thank God my dad was a better pilot than a mechanic!

Through the years, I have used various explanations while pleading for a safe outcome to a situation. Little did I know, I had already been assigned a guardian angel—and my guardian angel was starting to realize that this was not going to be an easy assignment.

My dad finally earned his commercial-instrument pilot rating and got a job with a small air taxi in Dillingham. He soon learned that in order to keep his first job as a bush pilot, he would need to take risks beyond what he was taught in flight school. The first time my dad was instructed to fly to the nearby village of Aleknagik in bad weather, he made it to within five miles of the airport before making a decision to turn around and return to Dillingham. When his new boss saw him taxi back to parking with the passengers still in the aircraft, he had a major meltdown. After yelling at my dad in front of the passengers for not making it to his destination, the owner of the small air taxi jumped into the plane and soon returned without the passengers. My dad never lived down the humiliation and vowed to himself that he would rather hit the ground than turn around.

Looking back, I can't recall my dad ever again returning to base without completing his objective because of weather; however, he did in fact hit the ground with five passengers aboard about three miles from Togiak Airport while flying from a high-pressure area to a low-pressure area, giving validity to the saying he was taught in flight school: "High to low, look out below." He was flying a Piper PA-34 Seneca. A Seneca is a low-wing twin-engine retractable-gear aircraft with a wingspan of about thirty-eight feet and an overall length of around twenty-eight feet. My dad was flying over Togiak Bay in a snowstorm in the middle of the winter, so he wasn't able to see anything but white at the time. He was hoping to see the dark houses of the village as he approached it. He was intending to land at the airport, which at the time literally stretched through the village.

Back then, there wasn't any way to get atmospheric pressure readings for airports other than those with flight service stations, like Dillingham. Airports that had flight service stations had meteorologists onsite, but unfortunately, when the flight service station was closed, there wasn't any automated weather reporting like there is today.

The aircraft altimeter was indicating five hundred feet at the time. My dad had a feeling he was getting close to Togiak, so he began to slow down and decided to lower the landing gear. As he did so, the wheels lowered into the snow, and the plane came sliding to a stop in the middle of Togiak Bay. No one was seriously injured, and the experience didn't seem to alter his bullheadedness. In fact, by this time in his life, mission-itis was a part of who he was.

Sometimes my dad would talk about his legs shaking on occasion while cheating death flying through some mountain pass barely big enough to fit through in weather most of us wouldn't go outdoors in. As a young boy, I took my dad's comments about his legs shaking to mean that you couldn't consider yourself a bush pilot unless you'd had at least one of your legs shaking uncontrollably while you used your superior skill to get you out of some jam your judgment obviously failed you on. Later in life, when I started jamming myself up in various situations involving aircraft and boats, I started to realize that it wasn't as much fun as he had made it sound.

I have often wondered how I ended up making my living flying airplanes. Sometimes I think it was because my family was always doing something fun that involved airplanes. The second company my dad eventually started flying for would let him borrow airplanes on occasion. I often had the opportunity to stand on my dad's lap and steer various aircraft using only the aileron and elevator. The aileron is a hinged flight-control surface usually forming part of the trailing edge of each wing. It is used in pairs to control the aircraft in roll around the longitudinal axis. The elevator, usually at the rear of an aircraft, controls the aircraft's pitch.

I was too short to reach the pedals for the rudder, a hinged control surface mounted on the vertical stabilizer. The rudder can be moved side to side with the pilot's feet and legs and plays a big role in a coordinated turn. In the air, you can fly an aircraft with aileron and elevator, but it won't be as smooth or coordinated without the addition of the rudder.

My favorite airplane my dad let me fly was one he would borrow on special summer weekends to take family and friends out to the Walrus Islands to view walruses. It was an amphibious 1942 Grumman Goose designed to serve as an eight-seat commuter aircraft for businessmen. During World War II, the Goose became an effective transport for the US military. It was approximately thirty-eight feet long, with a wingspan of forty-nine feet. It was pulled along by two 450-horsepower radial engines that sounded like a whole group of motorcycles rumbling down the road. My dad would let me steer the old girl as she rumbled out across Bristol Bay to land in the ocean next to the island and taxi up onto the beach.

On numerous occasions, my dad would let me steer his personal 160-horsepower, four-place, high-wing, tricycle-gear PA-22 Piper Tri-Pacer that was approximately twenty feet in length and had a twenty-nine-foot wingspan. We would often fly out to the beach to pick up the glass balls that would show up from time to time. Presumably, they had come all the way from Japan's coastline, where glass balls were commonly used as buoys associated with fishing nets. In the late sixties and early seventies, you could still find small and large glass balls, some still wrapped in the rope used to restrain them. Small glass balls still occasionally wash out of the banks along the coastline after big storms.

Walruses that die during the summer end up washed up onto the beach as well after a strong onshore wind. It is legal to harvest the tusks, teeth, and Oosik of a walrus that washes up on the beach dead. An *Oosik*, pronounced "oo, sik," is the Eskimo word for the walrus penis bone. Most people harvesting the walrus will take the entire head and the Oosik. A non-native person may keep the ivory if they register the ivory with fish and wildlife within thirty days. I'm not sure if that was a law back then or not.

As far back as I can remember, our family in one way or another made a living in the flying industry. And while that is undoubtedly one of the reasons I wound up in this line of work, I have also been exposed to plenty of reasons *not* to get into aviation. For example, in June 1966, my dad departed from Nushagak Point Beach with his PA-22 and struck his left main on an old piling left behind from an old dock. The aircraft launched into the air and settled into the bay.

When I listened to my dad telling the story later, the plane crash was incidental to the fact that he had barely made it to shore because of his inability to swim. Apparently my uncle and aunt were much better swimmers because they were able to get their two small children and themselves to shore safely. Drowning was something that everyone in Bristol Bay understood. When you were raised around the commercial fishing industry, it wasn't uncommon for someone you had seen before and possibly even knew to drown.

When an airplane has a tail wheel, it is normally referred to as a *taildragger*. In September 1968, there was another small airplane accident that sticks in my memory. Back then, Dillingham still had a small private airport that was close to town. On approach at night, a PA-20—which is a similar airplane to the PA-22 in size but was designed as a taildragger—struck a power line that ran across the end of the airport. The plane crash was not fatal, but one of the two men on board was seriously injured. Our family knew the man well because we were all members of the same Seventh-Day Adventist church.

One airplane crash that I will always remember was in December 1968. I was attending the Seventh-Day Adventist school in Dillingham. One early afternoon, we were all sitting at our desks when the preacher came into the classroom. We could tell he was upset, and we all knew that something bad had happened. The preacher singled my friend out and told him to gather up his things—he was going home for the day. Our teacher left the classroom with them and soon returned with the news that an aircraft had crashed near Pedro Bay and that thirty-six people had lost their lives. The aircraft was a Fairchild F-27, a high-wing, twin-engine turboprop passenger aircraft that was approximately eighty-three feet long with a wingspan of ninety-five feet. My friend lost his parents that day.

Another way I had been exposed to the dangers associated with flying airplanes was through my dad and his brother. They were always going out to crash sites and retrieving aircraft carcasses. Sometimes all they needed to do was beat a propeller back to where it wouldn't shake the engine completely off its mounts and then bring it home. Other times, their work was a bit more in-depth. Back then, most people couldn't afford to call in a helicopter to sling the aircraft back to where repairs could be completed, so either you cobbled it back together and brought it home yourself, or you got my dad and his brother to get it back for you. In some cases, it could be retrieved by boat or snowmobile, but if that didn't work, you had to leave it out in the field.

The back country of Alaska is riddled with twisted metal that once flew to that very spot and is now just someone's story, slowly fading away. My uncle's yard was always full of wrecked airplanes—presumably airplanes he was going to rebuild someday. We used to play in those airplanes all the time. Sometimes we would find blood and know someone had gotten hurt, possibly even killed, in the accident.

Despite all the dangers, the one thing that stood out in my mind was the heroics. I began to conclude that all I had to do to be a hero was become a bush pilot.

Chapter 2

MY DAD AND HIS GUARDIAN ANGEL

By the age of nine, I was fully aware of the possibility that people could lose their lives flying airplanes. However, I never thought for a minute it could happen to my dad.

In late September 1970, my dad was missing for several days. In a situation like that, praying doesn't seem like enough to do. If prayer is all you have though, you get down on your knees and pray until your legs go numb. That fall, my dad and his guardian angel went up against overwhelming odds. This is how I heard the story.

My dad had borrowed my uncle's four-seat, single-engine, high-wing Cessna 172, which was approximately twenty-seven feet in length, with a wingspan of thirty-six feet. The Cessna 172 was pulled along by a 160-horsepower engine. My dad borrowed the airplane to fly into Anchorage. He had scheduled only one night in Anchorage because of limited funds.

He flew into Anchorage on September 26, spent the night, and the next morning accomplished his business. In those days, there was very little information about the weather through mountain passes, so most of your weather came from other pilots who would attempt to fly through a pass and then call back their report as soon they either made it through or turned back because of bad weather. When he called the flight service station to check the weather through the mountain pass that was the most direct route from Anchorage to Dillingham, named Lake Clark Pass, there were numerous pilot reports that the pass was closed. My dad was forced to spend another night in Anchorage.

Anyone who knew my dad would tell you that he didn't have the patience to just hang around and wait for the weather to get better. Early the next day, he decided to go and look at the weather in the pass for himself. This was just his way of saying, *I'm going home regardless of the weather.* He made it to the entrance to the pass and was able to identify it as being the correct entrance. He then proceeded around the first sharp turn to the right. There is a short straightaway that follows the first sharp corner. At the end of the straightaway, there is an opportunity to turn around.

Most of the mountain passes in Alaska aren't wide enough for small airplanes to turn around and go back anytime they want. Instead, there are usually opportunities throughout the pass to turn around. I was always taught by pilots other than my dad not to commit yourself to flying completely through a mountain pass; rather, commit yourself to flying from one turnaround location to another until you reach the end.

This particular opportunity to turn around was Dad's last until he crossed the next obstacle, which was a glacier that in the seventies extended all the way across the bottom of the pass. In a snowstorm, the glacier was very difficult to cross because of the whiteout conditions you would encounter, making this area the most dangerous to get through. He knew that once he cleared the glacier, he would have the worst behind him.

Encouraged by the thought of only needing to get through this one dangerous location, combined with a case of what is known in Alaska as get-home-itis, he continued. As he reached the glacier, he lost all contact with the ground. Instinctively, he jerked the control wheel back hard and found himself in a steep climb.

Lake Clark Pass Glacier

The Cessna 172 has a stall warning indicator, which is basically a horn that goes off when the aircraft approaches the speed at which the aircraft will no longer fly. He told me later that he was climbing at such a steep angle that the stall warning horn was blaring the whole time. He realized the second he pulled that control back that he was committed to climb out between the mountains. There is no changing your mind when you do something like that. All he could do was sit there praying out loud for God's protection.

At about 4,500 feet, he began thinking that he was going to clear the mountains, but at 5,000 feet he smashed into the rocks. His head flew forward, driving his forehead into the dash. The altimeter knob stuck out from the dash about a quarter of an inch and was now driven deep into his forehead. His head hit the knob with such force, it broke a chunk out of his skull bone. Telling the story later, he would stop at this point and let me feel the chunk of bone that would move just under the skin. Listening to him describe the events following the impact, I realized once again that the dramatic part of the story was not the crash itself but the events that were to follow.

He did not have much in the way of survival equipment, just a pocket knife and some groceries he had purchased in Anchorage—the kind of things that were too expensive to get in Dillingham, like fresh vegetables, cheese, milk, and fruit. He grabbed what he could carry and begin climbing down the mountain. It was very windy, and before he got very far, he saw the plane slide and tumble down into a ravine, out of sight.

He told me that just before dark, he came upon a glacier. Because glaciers are constantly moving, it was making lots of noise, and he was scared to proceed down the glacier at night. He found some rocks to crouch down into out of the wind and held there until first light.

The next morning, he made his way down the glacier through small tunnels with freezing cold water flowing through them, jumping over cracks in the glacier. This must have been quite a sight because I've seen my dad jump. He wasn't very agile; in fact, he was quite stiff. He told me that not knowing where to step in the areas that were still covered in snow was probably the scariest because he wasn't sure when a hole was going to open and drop him inside.

Once he made it through all that, there was the thick alder to forge through. Alders are only about ten to fifteen feet tall, but they grow like vines and stretch out in all directions, so you must step over some branches and crawl under others, all the while climbing down a steep mountain full of boulders the size of your recliner.

Finally, he made it to the bottom and out into the valley. But he did not have any means of making a fire. He didn't have any protection from the nine-foot-tall brown bears that were trying to fatten up for the long hibernation period ahead. He proceeded to make a shelter that would allow him to keep a close eye out for any approaching aircraft that might be looking for him, as well as any hungry bear that might be looking for an easy meal.

He had now been missing for a little over twenty-four hours. My mom kept my sister and I calm with prayer and encouraging words. She tried to hide the fact that deep down inside, she feared the worst, based on the simple fact that typically when someone went missing in an airplane, the outcome was rarely good. When my sister and I went to school the next day, several of our classmates kept telling us that our dad was probably dead. They relentlessly reinforced their theory with statistics from the past. That was a rough day at school, and in the spirit of faith and positivity, my mom said we didn't have to go back until my dad was home safe.

For the first time in my short life, I feared for my dad's life. No one had been able to get into the pass—not even the Coast Guard Rescue HH-60 Jayhawk helicopter that was sixty-four feet long and cruised along at 160 miles per hour. All the Coast Guard could do was circle overhead in the ninety-seven-foot-long Lockheed C-130 Hercules with a wingspan of 132 feet, its four turboprop engines echoing the sweet sound of hope and encouragement, only to be drowned out by the vastness of the mountain range.

The C-130 is a military transport aircraft that is widely used in Alaska for search and rescue. The Coast Guard base is in Kodiak, located on Kodiak Island on the south coast of Alaska about two hundred miles from where my dad crashed. As they circled overhead, they listened to the ELT (emergency location transmitter), hoping that my dad would have the ability to use the aircraft radio, which would verify that he was alive. But because his aircraft was on top of a five-thousand-foot mountain, he had no means of communication. If satellite phones were used somewhere in the world in the early seventies, they sure weren't used by your average Alaskan, nor were cell phones.

Finally, on the 30th, planes could get into the pass, but they were limited to searching the base of the pass because of the low ceilings and poor visibility. My mom rode with my uncle in one of his other airplanes, and at one point they flew directly over my dad. He later told me he tried to hit the airplane with a rock, but it was a little too high in the air. There was no luck finding him that day, but the next day when the Coast Guard helicopter came up the pass, he got their attention. They landed and picked him up. Aside from the dried blood on his face and clothing, he was in surprisingly good shape and spirits.

To this day, the airplane has never been found, despite efforts by my dad and his friends. They would search for the plane whenever they had an opportunity, mostly out of curiosity as to where he had actually run into the mountain. After my dad safely returned home, I recall him reliving the story with his friends. One of the guys said jokingly, "Boy, Phil, your guardian angel really came through for you this time!" It would be a few years before I appreciated the meaning of those words.

Chapter 3

A YOUNG BOY AND HIS ANGEL

In the early seventies, my parents bought an existing air taxi company they eventually named Yute Air Alaska. *Yute* is a Yupik Eskimo expression for "the people's." It was my parents' intent to name their company "The People's Air Alaska."

Growing up in the air taxi business, I had plenty of opportunity to ride with pilots as they went about their daily activities hauling mail, freight, and people. I enjoyed flying, and I knew how by learning everything I could from the pilots I flew with. My goal was to someday be just like the heroic bush pilots I had idolized my entire life. Looking back, I can pinpoint the exact moment when I knew I was on the right path to become the bush pilot I had always dreamed about being.

It was a clear, cold winter day, somewhere around twenty degrees below zero. My dad came to me and said, "Come on. You're coming with me to Togiak." Togiak is a small village on the coast of Bristol Bay and is located at the head of Togiak Bay, sixty-seven miles west of Dillingham. It lies near what is now the Togiak National Wildlife Refuge, and it is the gateway to Walrus Island Game Sanctuary. Winter temperatures range from forty-five degrees below zero to thirty degrees above.

There is a mountain range that lies between Togiak and Dillingham. The mountains are anywhere from 1,200 feet to 2,700 feet above sea level. When we arrived at Togiak, we pulled up in front of the most beautiful piece of equipment I had ever seen. It was a little airplane painted completely yellow except for a sleek black stripe that started out skinny near the tail and ended in a Z-like pattern that was about two inches wide just behind the engine. On the tail, there was a decal of a little bear cub holding a sign that said CUB. The engine's cylinder heads stuck out of the cowling on both sides, and you could see two exhaust pipes coming out of the engine and then back into the cowling before appearing again on the bottom. The prop had a little yellow cap covering the bolts that held it on.

The flight controls were simple. They consisted of a metal pipe that came up out of the floor between your legs and controlled the aileron and elevator, referred to as a *stick*. It also had pedals for your feet that controlled the rudder. I had seen airplanes that looked similar but nothing exactly like this.

I asked my dad what it was, and he told me that it was a 1939 Piper J-3 Cub. I asked him what the coat-hanger-size rod I could see sticking out of the area just behind the engine was, and he told me it was a fuel-quantity indicator for the twelve-gallon gas tank. He said the rod I could see sticking up had a floating cork attached to the bottom end that would float on top of the gas; when the small rod was as far down as it could go, you were out of fuel.

He also told me that the airplane only weighed 765 pounds and was approximately twenty-two feet long, with a wingspan of thirty-five feet. The engine had been modified from sixty-five horsepower to eighty-five. Instead of wheels and tires, it had skis that were buried about six inches under the ice. We worked for an hour chopping that little plane's homemade skis out of the ice.

I later found out that someone in the village owed the air taxi a significant amount of money, and my dad had taken the aircraft in trade for the debt. I don't recall how we got that little aircraft engine heated up, but knowing my dad, he probably found some piece of tin and used it to direct heat from a small fire beneath the engine. What I do remember is that when we finally got that engine started and the little Cub free from the ice, he put me in the front seat.

We slid out onto the snow-covered runway. You could tell I was smiling even from the back side of my head. I had the stick gripped firmly in my right hand; my left hand and my short fat fingers were wrapped around the wooden ball that was the sliding throttle arm. It was as if that little wooden ball had been manufactured just for my hands.

The J-3 Cub, like most small airplanes, had a way of heating the carburetor. It was a system used in piston-powered light-aircraft engines to prevent clear carburetor icing. It consisted of a movable flap that draws hot air into the engine intake. The air was drawn from the heat stove, a metal plate around the very hot exhaust manifold.

It was so cold that day that my dad instructed me to slowly advance the throttle to the full power position with the carburetor heat on. Once the throttle was advanced, I used my thumb to push in the carburetor heat control mechanism. I had the stick all the way back, and by now all eighty-five horses were galloping down the runway as fast as they could go. Instinctively, I looked as far down the runway as I could and kept the airplane going straight with my happy feet—my way of saying I moved the rudder back and forth with my legs and feet in such a way that the rudder movements kept the little Cub going straight down the middle of that runway.

The order soon came from the back seat to release some of the back pressure, and as I did that, the little Cub eased into the air. This was my first flight in that little yellow Cub. I was flying! The feelings I experienced on that one-hour flight back to Dillingham at three hundred feet through the mountains on that cold winter day will be a part of who I am for as long as I live. That little yellow J-3 Cub and I were like two peas in a pod.

The Cub eventually became more like a prosthetic limb than an aircraft. I wouldn't just fly that little cub—I would strap it on. My dad used to come home from work dragging his hind end from flying all day under God only knows what conditions. I would meet him as he got out of his truck and beg to go flying. Rarely would he say no. We didn't always get to go up for long, but often we got to go up. It was convenient, at least in the winter, because we were able to park the plane in front of our house. With old blankets, extension cords, and a car heater, I was able to have the airplane ready for him when he got home.

Eventually, after I reached a certain level of ability, my dad would allow me to take the Cub out by myself. I was not yet of age to solo, but our house was on the edge of a square mile of open vegetation composed of dwarf shrubs, sedges, grasses, mosses, and lichens, with no trees—commonly known as tundra. I could fly in ground effect, which is the increased lift force and decreased aerodynamic drag that an aircraft's wings generate when they are close to a fixed surface. When landing, ground effect can give a pilot the feeling that the aircraft is floating. When taking off, ground effect may temporarily reduce the stall speed. The pilot can then fly just above the runway while the aircraft accelerates in ground effect until a safe climb speed is reached. When I ran out of room, I would just put a ski on the ground and turn around, half flying, half taxiing.

This worked out great until one day I broke the cardinal rule: absolutely under no circumstances was I allowed to have any of my cousins anywhere around when I was exercising my privileges. I don't know what my thought process was when I broke this unbreakable rule, but I was sitting in the parking spot with the engine running with my cousin sitting in the back seat. My dad came around the corner in his truck and drove up alongside us on the left. My cousin opened the door that was on the right, jumped out, and started running as fast as he could toward his house.

I, on the other hand, didn't know what to do. I shut the engine off and was contemplating running. My dad must have figured I would run, so he reached through the plexiglass window that was on the side he drove up on and grabbed me by the shoulders. It was cold that day, and the plexiglass shattered into pieces like ice. He pulled me through what was left of the window, and when I hit the ground, he proceeded to give me a good full body beating with his belt. I assume it was his belt—I didn't get a good look because I was busy squirming around trying to offer up new body parts to minimize the burning. He could have been using jumper cables for all I know. My dad was very creative with his beatings.

I ended up in a pile not more than thirty feet from the scene of the crime. I don't know why I wasn't grounded for life, but in a few weeks, after my bruises healed and I cut a new piece of plexiglass and repaired the window, I was back on the tundra practicing my high-speed taxi. At this stage in my life, I wasn't aware that I had a guardian angel who was with me every second of every day. Looking back, I can't help but think that my guardian angel must have been trying to warn me about breaking the cardinal rule.

Sadly, it wouldn't be until later in life that I started to read the signs my angel would put up in plain sight. Choosing to read those signs would take some harsh lessons at the school of hard knocks.

Chapter 4

MY ANGEL SHARED MY DREAM

My birthday was on July 7. From the age of two until the age of sixteen, I'd never had a single birthday on land. I had been on the water every summer. My parents no longer commercial-fished in the summer now that they owned Yute Air, but I continued to fish with one of my uncles. At age fifteen, I purchased a twenty-eight-foot fishing vessel and my grandpa's limited-entry commercial salmon fishing permit on credit I received through the Togiak cannery, and I was fishing in Togiak Bay.

My sixteenth birthday was going to be different. My parents and I had been planning the big day for years. The goal was for me to solo the J-3 Cub. My father, unbeknownst to me, had a backup plan. The day before my birthday, my dad came over to Togiak where I was fishing and picked me up in a 1970 Cessna 206.

The Cessna 206 or 207 is a single-engine general-aviation aircraft with fixed landing gear used in commercial air service and for personal use. The six-seat model 206 had a 285-horsepower engine, while the seven-seat 207 was forty-five inches longer and powered by a 300-horsepower engine. The 206 had a pilot-side door and large clamshell rear door on the right side serving the back two rows of seats, allowing easy loading of oversized cargo. The 207 had a small baggage compartment between the windshield and the engine and a door for both front seats, as well as the clamshell doors behind the wing on the right side.

The Cessna 206 was twenty-eight feet long and had a wingspan of thirty-six feet. I had been flying the 206 for about a year from the left seat whenever I was on a trip with my dad that had no passengers, or at least passengers that he knew well, which was just about everyone. He let me fly the airplane back to Dillingham from the left seat. We did some maneuvers on the way back.

That night, as you can imagine, I had a very sleepless night. I was used to praying to God only when I was in big trouble, but that night I made an exception. I even went so far as to kneel in front of my bed—something I hadn't done for a long time. At first light, after getting at least some sleep, I awoke to a beautiful sunny day. However, the wind was howling.

I was devastated. I had been planning this day in my mind for years. When my dad got up that morning, I pointed out the high wind. He assured me that I had nothing to worry about and to just relax and eat breakfast with the family. Easier said than done while choking down my own breakfast of disappointment and anxiety. I knew that flying the Cub in that wind was going to be impossible.

After breakfast, my dad and I headed out to the airport. Nothing seemed to be out of the ordinary. People were just going about their business, preparing their airplanes for the day. My dad didn't miss a beat. Upon our arrival at the airport, he pointed to the 206 and said, "Go preflight." I didn't know what to think. Was he saying this because I was going to hang out with him again all day, or was I actually going to solo that airplane in this wind? I rushed anxiously to the airplane and began to preflight.

When my mom and sister showed up with what looked like

a birthday cake, things started to get real. My dad, not being the kind of guy who wasted any time, soon climbed through the pilot-side door and shimmied behind the left seat and into the right while ordering me into the left. I was scared, excited, and nervous all at the same time.

Not only was the wind blowing that day, but as it turned out, it was a crosswind out of the east slightly favoring runway 01, which in plain English simply meant the airport ran north and south. Runway 01 would mean 010°, a runway you would be facing north on if you were taking-off or landing. An east wind would be coming at you from the right.

Runway 01 was turbulent down at the south end, especially with a strong east wind like the one we were experiencing. We went around the patch four times before my dad gave me the order to stop in the middle of the runway. He got up out of his seat, went to the back of the airplane, and opened the door. He jumped out and yelled back up to me, "Only three times, then get back to the hangar. We have work for this airplane today."

He locked the back door with his Allen wrench door key and never looked back. He just started walking back to the hangar. I couldn't help but smile nervously to myself as I shifted in my seat in preparation for takeoff. Oddly, even though my dad was no longer in the airplane, I didn't feel alone.

I took off crabbing profusely into the wind. My dad had a strict rule against trying to save a bad landing, and it was strictly prohibited to continue to land after bouncing in a crosswind. I was determined not to bounce. I had been given a huge opportunity to prove myself, and I wasn't about to disappoint myself or my dad. I limited my flaps to help keep my speed up and give me more control. The second my right gear touched the ground, I immediately slapped the electric flaps switch to the up position. The main gear touched down firmly, followed by the nose gear. I used the same technique on the other landings, and before I knew it, I was at the end of the third.

I did what I was told and taxied back to the parking spot in front of the hangar. The back of my T-shirt was immediately cut off, and the group of employees who had witnessed the flight signed the shirt. I was familiar with the tradition of cutting the back off the shirt a person wears when he solos, and I had worn a T-shirt I didn't mind ruining just in case.

The cake my mom and sister had made for me was a replica of my solo certificate. They even had frosting in a little bag for me to sign my name with. Pictures were taken to document the event before we all ate the cake. Later that day, I returned to Togiak to finish the summer season of commercial fishing, but I was a changed man—a pilot. I had a piece of paper in my pocket that said so.

I didn't get to fly again that summer until late September, when I finished fishing and returned home to my little yellow Cub. My dreams were nearly crushed that day. It was only by the grace of God and the determination of my family that my dream came true.

I have seen some nasty weather roll through Bristol Bay, and although the wind was blowing, it could have been a lot worse. When I got back to Togiak that night, I got back on my knees in the bow of my little wooden boat and thanked God for the way the day had turned out. I couldn't help but think about the feeling I had experienced while I soloed. It was at that moment that the statement about the guardian angel I had heard as a young boy made perfect sense. I realized that I hadn't been alone, and the epiphany of my guardian angel changed my life.

Chapter 5

I NAMED MY ANGEL JOE

I hadn't been back home from fishing more than a day when I was practically tipped over by a 112-foot-long Lockheed L-100 Hercules, the civilian variant of the prolific C-130 Hercules the military and Coast Guard use. I was in the pattern shooting touch-and-goes—landing but not stopping, rather getting back in the air instead. I was using the runway that had me facing south while taking off and landing, known as runway 19 (or 190° if you prefer). Flying without a radio was normal back then if you were flying an airplane that had been manufactured without an electrical system.

I was making several takeoffs and landings as I went from north to south down the runway. I was trying to get as many landings as I could on each run because of the long flight time from one end to the other. On one of my runs, I landed and started to take back off when I heard this rumbling sound. I pulled the power back, landed, and listened for a second before dismissing the noise as nothing important. I added power again and took off.

Just then, out my right window, I saw a Hercules L-100 barely above the ground on a go-around. The L-100 cut back in front of me and lined back up with the runway. Not reacting quickly enough to land, I flew right into his wake turbulence, and the Cub nearly flipped over. Before I knew it, I was at a ninety-degree angle thirty feet off the ground.

I pulled the stick back into my lap and shot out to the left, nearly hitting my uncle's aircraft repair shop. Knowing that I was in big trouble, I flew parallel to the runway to just past the end before making a 180-degree turn to the right and landing on the end of runway 01. My friend's dad had an old open-face hangar at the end of the runway, off in the trees. The taxiway leading to the hangar was not far from the end, but I managed to pull onto the taxiway and quickly pull into the hangar and shut the engine off. I hid there until the L-100 left.

At the time, my dad's company unloaded the L-100 whenever it came to Dillingham, and my dad was getting an earful about the little yellow Cub that had practically gotten itself run over. My dad knew exactly who was in the little yellow Cub, but he acted like he had no clue who could've been so stupid as to get in the way of a Hercules. After they left, I snuck back into my parking spot and was trying to tie the plane down as fast as I could to make my escape when my dad pulled up in his truck. He let me know that he had heard all about my little mishap. I was glad that he wasn't too upset about the whole thing. He was just glad that I hadn't been killed.

My dad had this theory about pilots. When people would do something stupid and end up losing their lives, he would say, "That's a mistake they won't be learning from." I had indeed lived and learned a valuable lesson, and my guardian angel had once again pulled me out of an ugly situation. The lesson I learned was about the importance of a radio. With Dillingham getting more and more traffic, this was increasingly significant.

I explained to my dad what had happened and talked to him

about maybe getting a handheld radio so something like this wouldn't happen again. He was from the old school and believed in looking out the window. He said, "Just because you're in a big airplane don't mean you don't have to look outside for other airplanes." The radio wasn't required for uncontrolled airspace like Dillingham if the clouds were higher than 1,000 feet above the ground and the visibility was greater than three miles.

Later that night, I thought about what my dad said, but the event had shaken me up enough that I promised myself I would consider buying a handheld radio, at least for the Dillingham airport. I still wanted to be old-school like my dad and others I had idolized my entire life, but I justified it in my mind that, out of courtesy to the other pilots, I would use the radio. It wasn't long, though, before I forgot all about needing a radio and was once again attempting to live my life old-school. I will tell you this: I will never forget the lesson I learned about wake turbulence.

I was now fully aware of my guardian angel and knew he was sent by God to protect me. I also knew that God was the one who would determine how long I stayed alive on earth and didn't hesitate to ask for help when I was in trouble. Just before I came home and was nearly turned into window-dressing for a Hercules, I had narrowly escaped death while fishing alone the last week of salmon season.

My twenty-eight-foot wooden skiff was old and some of the wood was getting soft—a nice way of saying rotten. The boat had a small cabin in the stern just in front of the two outboard motors, typical for Togiak Bay. The six-inch space between the cabin and the outer structure of the boat served as a walkway from the back of the boat (stern) to the front of the boat (bow). Because of the rotting wood in this area, it was slick. I had slipped on this section of the boat several times that summer.

Togiak Bay Fishing Vessel

My solution, which I had implemented before heading out to fish alone, was to nail a skinny strip of wood along the outer edge of this area of the boat. The nails were driven into the soft wood. I knew it was most likely not going to hold for long, but I was already looking for a different boat to fish the following year and was hopeful it would last the week.

A few days later, I was rushing up to the bow of the boat from the stern. I was wearing rubber boots that went up my legs to my hip, commonly called hip boots. I was also wearing a rain jacket and pants. I kept my cotton gloves in a bucket up in the bow, so I wasn't wearing any gloves. The piece of wood I had nailed on the edge gave way as I was rushing by.

I fell off the boat but managed to cling to rotten wood with just my fingers. I wasn't hanging onto much, but I managed to cling on for dear life. I knew that if I slipped into the forty-degree hypothermic water below, I would die. I had seen people fall into the water the way I was dressed, and after the initial splash, they never came back up.

I cried out to God, "Please, God, not here, not now"—a familiar prayer by this stage in my life. I could feel my boots filing up with water, and they were dragging me down. My fingers were very strong back then, especially at the end of the fishing season, but it still took everything I had to get past the cabin and to an area of the boat I could potentially climb in from.

I wasn't out of the woods yet. My boots were full of water, and I was running out of strength. Exhausted and with my fingers slowly losing their grip, I knew it was now or never. With all the stubbornness and determination I had inherited from my dad, I began to pull myself up. The harder I pulled, the more it felt as if my boots were full of helium rather than 8.3-pounds-a-gallon water. The extra boost was all I needed to get me up and over the side.

I was physically drained, and my hip boots were still full of water. I had to get the water out of my boots as quickly as possible because the reason I was rushing up to the bow in the first place was that my net was in danger of washing ashore onto the rocks. I had cut it loose from the boat and driven to the end closest to the rocks, where I was attempting to reconnect the net when I fell over. Now my boat was in danger of washing ashore, and it was imperative that I get to a motor and quick.

I managed to get most of the water out of my boots, but it still felt like I had water bottles hanging down from my knees. Despite the awkwardness of my hip boots drooping down, I managed to make my way to the stern. I had two outboard motors, fifty-five and twenty-five horsepower. They were bolted to the outside of the transom—the horizontal beam reinforcing the stern of the boat. A pull rope was mounted in front of each engine housing for easy access. Pulling the rope would turn the motor over for starting rather than having to use an electric starter. The mechanism for shifting gears was mounted on the side of the motor in easy reach.

The smaller motor always started on the first pull, so I went straight for it. About a week earlier, the safety that prevented the engine from turning over while in gear had broken—a small miracle because it enabled me to pull the shifting mechanism into forward thrust with my left hand and pull the rope with my right. The engine started as usual, and without looking at the rocks, I somehow got to the throttle as the boat was on its final lunge for certain disaster.

I went back out to the deep end of the net and did what I should have done in the first place. Once hooked back up, I towed it out into the deep water. You lose fish that way, but better them than me, I figured at that point.

That night, back on anchor, I thought about the event that had happened that day. Being raised a Christian, I was taught that all the hairs on our head are numbered. I guess I always thought that meant our lives were all mapped out, and we had an expiration date like yogurt or something. Subconsciously, I must not have accepted the fact that I had an expiration date because whenever I got myself in a jam, I called out to God.

I was also taught that when we give our lives to God and let him know we are willing vessels, our lives can be used in a much bigger plan than we can ever imagine. As I thought about the day's events, I hit my knees and did just that. Only by the grace of God and my guardian angel's help did I manage to pull myself over the edge of the boat, exhausted and with my boots full of water. It is comforting for me to believe that I have a guardian angel who is always with me, and if it doesn't interfere with God's plan, will help me whenever I need it. My recent brush with death had reinforced my belief in my own personal guardian angel, and it was on that very night that I named my angel Joe.

Chapter 6

BEAR HUNTING WITH MY ANGEL JOE

In late September 1977, I had only been back from fishing in Togiak Bay long enough to nearly get run over by a Hercules, and I was already planning a new adventure. That summer, my cousin who lived next door to me growing up had been my first mate. He was about six feet tall and 150 pounds, with sandy blond hair. He had the biggest grin of anyone I had ever seen. He was always in a good mood and had grown up working hard like me, so we had done quite well financially that summer.

Naturally, after working all summer, we were both ready to have some fun. We decided we were going bear hunting. I had overheard some local Togiak residents talking about a river called Izavieknik that summer—great bear hunting, they said. The Izavieknik River flowed between Upper Togiak and Togiak Lake. Upper Togiak Lake received water from the mountains and valleys that surrounded its upper end.

The Izavieknik had a small volume of water as it left the lake but increased in volume shortly after because of a small waterway called Trail Creek that drained a long wide valley. Trail Creek flowed in from the west and doubled the size of the Izavieknik. Other small rivers and creeks flow into the Izavieknik, and by the time the Izavieknik reached Togiak Lake, it was a very substantial river.

Togiak Lake is the headwaters of the Togiak River, which makes up most of the spawning ground for the salmon that return to the Togiak area every four years to repeat the cycle. The Togiak River is approximately seventy miles long and has many tributaries and creeks feeding it that also make great spawning habitats. I was certain that I knew exactly where the good bear hunting was supposed to be and that I could fly Little Yeller to that location.

My cousin and I started eagerly packing our bags for the trip. Because I only had a license to fly by myself, our plan—if you can call it that—was for me to taxi down to the departure end of runway 19 at Dillingham and pick up my cousin, who would be hiding in the bushes. He would have with him his two full-grown black labs. In an attempt to throw the scent off our trail, I told my dad that I was going to go out camping by myself. I told him I was going to Cinnabar Mine, a little abandoned mercury mine just east of Aleknagik Village with its own grass runway named Tripod.

Aleknagik is located at the head of the Wood River on the southeast end of Lake Aleknagik, sixteen miles northwest of Dillingham. Tripod runway was forty miles southeast of where we really intended to go. This wasn't the smartest thing a pilot could do to increase the odds of being found if something were to go wrong. We discussed the dangers and concluded that the odds of something going wrong were slim to none.

I loaded up our two backpacks and two guns in the back of Little Yeller and taxied down to where my cousin was hiding with his dogs. I opened the door, and they came rushing in. After a brief struggle with a dog who thought the front seat would be more comfortable, I advanced the throttle, and we were off. This

J-3 Cub had three fuel tanks: the main twelve-gallon fuel tank between the engine and the windshield and two wing tanks of fifteen and twenty gallons that someone had put in the wings illegally. Burning 4.5 gallons per hour, we had plenty of gas.

We ended up somewhere in the upper stretches of the Izavieknik River. As with everything I did back then, I had gotten off to a late start. By the time we reached our destination, it was starting to get dark. We were committed to finding somewhere to land along the river. We had not done any research as to where we were going to land, however, or even if we were going to be able to land. In fact, this was the poorest, most ill-conceived, most idiotic spur-of-the-moment idea ever. We just flew along the river until we spotted a stretch that, out of utter desperation, might suffice as a landing location. There were thirty- to forty-foot-tall trees on both sides of the river for miles in each direction. The only way to get down next to the river was to slip between the trees and touch down immediately.

A slip is an aerodynamic state in which an aircraft is moving somewhat sideways as well as forward relative to the oncoming airflow or relative wind. In other words, a slip is a cross-control maneuver that essentially lets the airplane descend at a higher rate without building speed. It was a common maneuver for the J-3 Cub because the plane wasn't designed with flaps, which are usually mounted on the wing trailing edges of a fixed-wing aircraft. Flaps are used to lower the minimum speed at which the aircraft can be safely flown and to increase the angle of descent for landing.

In this case, there was no gravel bar to waste. Desperate to get on the ground, I hadn't given any thought as to how we were going to get out of this hole I was landing in. The execution of what was no longer a plan but a knee-jerk reaction to the fear of dying that was threatening to paralyze my body lacked all finesse.

I slipped down between the trees with the throttle pulled back hard against the stop.

Immediately after touching down, I spotted a half-buried log across the middle of the landing field. There looked to be only enough room to comfortably squeeze my right wheel between the river and the log. At this point, I was committed, and there was no going around to try again. With my fingers squeezing the wooden throttle ball, I added power with my left arm and punched at the left rudder pedal with my left leg to keep us going straight while firmly thrusting the stick over to the right and back with my right arm to force the left wing up using aileron and elevator.

The left wheel lifted just enough to bounce off the top of the log before slamming back onto the beach. I pulled the power back again. Rapidly running out of room, I realized I had forgotten to put hydraulic fluid in my leaky left brake before we left Dillingham. To apply brakes, a pilot uses his heel to press on a brake pedal protruding out of the floor while both feet are on the rudder pedals. Faced with the reality of only having one workable brake on the right side, and now just about to roll out into the river, I crammed on the right brake with my heel and pulled the stick back and to the right. The tail of the Cub switched places with the nose, and the momentum of the tail slinging around pulled us out into the current of the river.

The power of the river was pulling us in, and I could feel us starting to slip out into the water. The prop was still barely out of the water as I added full power and crawled back up onto the beach. Shaken but still alive, we jumped out to inspect the airplane. The only obvious damage was to the left elevator. We pushed the plane back into the trees to tie it down for the night, and as we were doing so, I noticed that the left tire had gravel packed between wheel and tire. Because it was getting late, we decided to make camp and assess our situation in the morning.

Neither one of us know a single thing about bear hunting. Looking back, I don't think two shotguns with slugs were the best choice of weapons. That night, we slept with one eye open, praying we wouldn't be visited by the one thing that only hours before we had been praying to see.

The next day, after a breakfast of bacon, eggs, and regret, we assessed our situation. The first thing we did was walk down to the beach to see if we could clear enough driftwood to make a successful getaway. We had already planned to spend the rest of our hunting trip trying to get ourselves out of the mess we were in. The log that was right in the middle of our departure wouldn't budge. Frankly, we couldn't figure out how we had missed it while we were landing.

We removed sticks and debris off to the side of the stretch of beach we were going to use as a runway. Thankfully, the water had come down enough overnight that we'd have enough room to squeeze by the log we couldn't move. Now my dilemma was, what would we leave behind? Promising that I would come back and pick up our guns, camping equipment, and packs, we decided to stash everything in the trees. We then turned our attention to the bent elevator. We were able to straighten it fairly well with little effort. As it turned out, it wasn't made of real heavy material, so although it looked bad, it straightened up quite nicely.

We couldn't do anything about the gravel threatening to pop our tire, so we just chose to ignore it. I taxied the Cub back as far as we could go, and as we had hoped, we were able to fit between the river and the log. We jumped out of the Cub and pulled it back as far as we could. In fact, the tail wheel was in the river. We loaded up the two dogs, started the Cub, and then took a minute to pray. Feeling confident that we served a merciful and forgiving God, we began our takeoff roll. We made it around the log and continued down the gravel bar.

It looked like we were heading for a dead end because all we could see were the trees on the other side of the river directly in front of us. The river ran perpendicular to our takeoff path before it made a hairpin turn to the right. The turn wasn't visible from our position, and we had no idea what was around the first corner. Frankly we were concentrating so hard on the landing the previous night that neither one of us could say with any certainty what was in store for us.

As the wheels left the ground at the end of the gravel bar, I could hear my dad saying, "Don't stop flying until the plane is tied down." With the throttle hard against the stops, I convinced that little Cub to make a left turn just before slamming into the trees. With the wing practically in the water, I cranked hard to the right. Around the corner, still feet above the water, we got our first break—a straightaway. Soon we were above the trees and on our way home. I took a deep breath and thanked God for sparing our lives.

Of course, I still had the extra passenger and two dogs to get rid of. When we arrived back in the Dillingham area, I could tell by the planes we observed taking off and landing that they were using runway 01. I needed runway 19 to do the reverse of our getaway. With no radio, my plan was to land on the end of 19, turn around, and take off on 01. All this would be done at the bottom of the slight hill that started about in the middle of the 6,000-foot runway and sloped down to the north, giving the north end of the runway just enough cover for me to execute my plan. I would then fly a normal tragic pattern, hoping that no one would be the wiser.

Confident that anyone seeing my odd behavior would dismiss it as me being a nuisance as usual, I started to execute my well-thought-out plan. I landed as close to the end of 19 as I could. Unfortunately, when I touched down, the left tire popped from all the gravel packed in it. Luckily, the extra drag on the left main was easily countered with the right brake I still had, and we came to a stop without further incident.

My cousin opened the door and jumped out, with the two dogs jumping at the same time. Luckily, neither of the dogs ran forward because I had elected not to shut the engine off. I had no choice but to limp back to the hangar uphill. I would just have to hope for the best—a familiar theme on this trip. As luck would have it, my dad was landing on runway 01 as I cleared at the taxiway to the north of the ramp. He cleared at the taxiway to the south of the ramp and beat me back to the hangar.

I really couldn't say much—nor did I have the opportunity. My dad had already put two and two together and had pretty much figured everything out except for where the crash had occurred. Filling in the gaps wasn't really necessary because at the time, he really didn't want my input. After my chewing-out, I slithered off in an old van that belonged to the company to join up with my partner in crime. He had also filled in the blanks and was hightailing it home to neutral territory. I eventually caught up with him, and like a couple of squirrels chasing their tails, we tried to figure out where our adventure had gone wrong.

Over the years, I have flown up and down the Izavieknik River. Not only have I never found the spot where we camped, I haven't been able to even find a spot along the river where I would be willing to land. I know in my heart that it was our two guardian angels that kept us alive on that trip. Needless to say, our packs and guns are still there. After that, I decided it was probably best that I flew alone until I got my private license.

I ended up using some of my hard-earned fishing money to repair the Cub. It wasn't the first lesson I had learn the hard way, but this one hurt the worst for some reason. I suspect it was because I lied to my dad, put our lives in danger, and hurt my little yellow friend.

Chapter 7

NO REST FOR MY ANGEL

Before long, I strapped Little Yeller on and headed for Cape Constantine Beach. Cape Constantine is the most southerly point on the Nushagak Peninsula, and defines the southern side of Kulukak Bay. The beach is approximately forty miles long, and I would land on every land-able surface of it.

I flew out to the beach every chance I got until the snow got too deep to land. I would look for glass balls, walrus tusks, and whatever else I could find. I would fly mostly in ground effect like I did in front of our house before I was old enough to solo. I would run my wheels along the beach, jumping creeks. I worked for my dad doing whatever he wanted me to do, and in trade I would fill up my tanks. I had plenty of gas and tried my best to use it all.

One day on my way to the beach, I came across an area that had lots of ducks. I soon discovered that the ducks could fly at about 65 miles per hour—the same speed as the Cub. I tried to join the formation, but they would break up into small groups. I started chasing small groups in hopes they would let me fly with them. They weren't having anything to do with that.

I soon discovered that I could eventually wear them out, and I could fly in formation with them until they started to noticeably lather and lose altitude. At that time, I would salute them and let them go. I hate to admit it, but chasing ducks become an obsession of mine. Whenever I would head to the beach, I would stop for a little formation flying with the ducks.

It wasn't always calm winds and beautiful weather at the beach. One day while flying down the beach toward an area called Picnic at the extreme northwest end of Cape Constantine, I encountered increasingly strong winds that soon turned into severe turbulence. I was beside a small cliff, but the majority of the turbulence was coming from the mountains out to the northwest. Instinctively, I made an immediate turn to the left, hoping to get away from the cliff. Within seconds, I was in a relatively smooth air, and I made a 180-degree turn back toward the beach. It soon became apparent that I had gotten pushed out to sea way farther than expected. In cruise power, I was making very little headway back toward the beach.

I was also tracking easterly—not wanting to get back into the turbulence, but mostly because the beach to the right of me was angling in my favor, so I felt that even though I wasn't making much forward headway, I would be over land sooner tracking to the east. I probably had six gallons left in the nose tank—enough for about one hour and fifteen minutes at cruise power.

My fuel gauge was a metal rod with a cork attached to the end that was down in the twelve-gallon tank. The top half-inch of the rod was bent at a 90-degree angle to keep it from disappearing down into the tank when it was low on gas. The method used for filling the nose tank was to open a valve in the cockpit, which would allow fuel to gravity-feed down into the nose tank and fill it.

After what seemed like an hour, but in reality was probably more like fifteen minutes, I was getting pretty nervous. Being a Christian, I instinctively started praying: "Dear Jesus, please keep

my engine running and get me back over land as soon as possible."
I turned on the left fuel valve and started to fill the nose tank. At
least I wouldn't run out of gas.

It's funny the things that pop into your head when you are in
a pickle. I'm sure I had plenty of gas in my nose tank to get me
over the shore, but I hated just sitting there doing nothing. I'm
glad the old eighty-five-horsepower Continental didn't quit; it
would have been curtains for me. The further I sidetracked away
from the cliff, the more progress I made. Eventually, I made it
back over the beach.

I figured that was enough excitement for one day and started
heading for home. The downside to gravity-feeding fuel from a
large tank into a smaller tank is that you have to remember to
shut the valve back off. Gas soon began to pour down onto the
floor by my feet. Let's just say I'm glad I could open the window
and door while flying. As I headed back across the tundra toward
Dillingham, I could see that the clouds were lower than they were
when I left.

The clouds had a dark gray appearance to them, and I could
tell just by the way they looked that the visibility wasn't going
to be very good. I decided to track toward the east, hoping that
with the reduced visibility, following the beach would allow me
to get back to Dillingham safely. I made it to an area of the beach
where a river dumped in from the west called Snake River. From
Snake River on into Dillingham, there wasn't anywhere to land
a small plane because the coastline is made up of swampy grass
and tidal mudflats.

As I progressed, the visibility continued to get worse, and
it was getting hard to tell where the coastline ended and the
mudflats began. I turned around not knowing exactly what I
was going to do, but I wasn't comfortable continuing on toward

Dillingham. As I backtracked along the coastline, I realized I could see five miles across the bay over to Clark's Point Village.

Clark's Point Village had an airport that started at the beach and ran toward the east. I decided to make a beeline across the five-mile stretch of water to Clark's Point Airport before the weather got any worse. The clouds wouldn't allow me to climb very high, so I elected to stay low and get across the water as quickly as possible.

I had just spent thirty minutes over the water earlier in the day, so I figured that five more minutes wasn't going to make much of a difference. Thankful for my angel's comforting presence, I spent some time talking to Joe on the way across the last five miles to safety. I got within two miles of the shore before it started to snow. It was only snowing lightly, so I could still see the large cannery buildings, and I knew the airport was just to the right of them.

The closer I got, the harder it began to snow. By the time I reached the end of the airport, I was in the middle of a major snowstorm. Not to mention that by now, it was getting dark. Five more minutes, and I shudder to think how my day would have ended.

The storm lasted two days, but at least I was safe on the ground. The village had telephones, so I was able to stay in contact with my family. I stayed with some good friends of mine who lived near the airport, which was great because I could keep an eye on my airplane.

I had lots of these types of adventures in the Cub I called Little Yeller. One day I decided to get a close look at a mother bear and her two cubs. It was exciting, buzzing down over the bears, putting them right under my wing so that I could get a good look at them—but when the mother bear started standing up and swatting at me as a came by, I started to rethink what I was doing. I didn't have a gun I could carry with me, so I decided to hightail it out of the area before fate forced me down beside an angry mother bear.

That experience gave me a new and healthier respect for bears. From then on, when I landed on the beach to pick up glass balls or cut the head off a dead walrus, I would start to feel vulnerable and rush back to the airplane. I would then fly around looking over the area for any sign of bears, and then land and continue what I was doing. I was pretty confident that nothing was going to sneak up on me as long as I continued to survey the area.

Chapter 8

MY ANGEL THINKS OF EVERYTHING

Tundra Area I learned Ski Flying

Once the snow got too deep to land on the beach, I would hang around nearby airports and pray that the snow would get deep enough to put my old wooden skis on. Ski flying opened up a whole new world for me, as well as new territory to explore.

In the winter, Wood-Tikchik State Park was my playground. I flew as much as I could, juggling school and work, not flying as much as I would have liked. I learned a few things about ski flying that I hadn't learned in the flat area in front of the house. For example, I learned that you can get an airplane very stuck in deep snow. You hear stories about people having heart attacks while trying to get their airplane unstuck out in the wilderness. I was young and my heart was healthy, but I could certainly see how it could happen.

I also learned that a metal fifty-five gallon drum can be buried in just under the surface of the snow and that when you hit one with a ski on takeoff, it will ruin your day. I learned this lesson about thirty-five miles north of Dillingham, taking off from Okstukuk Lake in Wood-Tikchik State Park.

One beautiful sunny day, I was flying up in the park, chasing wolves and just generally buzzing around. I got a little cold, so I decided to stop at a cabin and warm up. Most cabins out away from civilization are open and generally have wood chopped up and stacked by the stove for people to use if they are out on their snowmobile and get caught in weather or it starts running late.

I started a fire and then chopped and stacked wood for the next guy. After warming up for a bit in front of the woodstove, I decided to head back to town. As I started my takeoff roll, I struck something solid just beneath the surface of the snow. I didn't know it at the time, but it was a fifty-five gallon drum. With the sun shining on the white snow, I didn't notice that the snow was slightly humped up over the drum.

The jolt from hitting the drum launched me into the air. Judging from the degree of impact, I suspected that I had done some damage to the ski. I got the Cub up to about three hundred feet, and because the impact was on the right side, I was able to open the door and lean out to look for damage. I rotated the aircraft along the longitudinal axis, and my suspicions were confirmed ... only it wasn't the ski that was broken, it was the landing gear. It was the peace that kept the gear from doing the splits on landing.

I was thankful to be airborne and decided to take the Cub home and land in front of the house. I expected further damage when I attempted to land, and I figured that in front of my parents' house would be a good spot to leave the airplane until it could be fixed. When I got to the tundra in front of the house, I lined up on a well-used snowmobile trail that led practically up to the front door. I touched down on the left ski and began to slow down. As the airplane settled onto the right ski, I reached up and turned the mags off. I was trying to protect the engine, but even better, the prop stopped in the vertical position instead of horizontal.

As the Cub started to do the splits, the wing dropped down onto the snow, and the Cub tried to tip over. Because the snow was so well compacted, the prop was now serving as a brake. The cub stayed upright, and the plane came to a stop. You could shut the engine off a thousand times and never have it stop straight down. I tell you what—Joe thinks of everything. I am truly blessed to have Joe as my guardian angel. He's the best.

I climbed out to assess the damage. From what I could see, the propeller was bent, and the bow of the wing tip was broken. There wasn't any further damage to the gear. There was only one thing to do: call my dad.

My dad soon showed up with his chief mechanic. The mechanic went right to work assessing the damage. He then left to gather up some parts he needed to get the plane off the tundra. He was able to borrow a prop and a gear leg. When he returned, he assigned me the task of duct-taping the wing tip.

My dad's company had grown to a fleet size of about thirty-five airplanes of various types. Periodically, he would throw these fits that people who worked for him would call Phil Attacks. My dad was six feet tall and had weighed 235 pounds most of his adult life. He had dark curly hair and at some point in his life he had gotten his lower front teeth knocked out and replaced with false teeth. He would unconsciously lift his false teeth up and down using his tongue whenever he was upset. I referred to this as flicking his teeth. He always wore well-broken-in work clothes that somehow helped reinforce an air he had about him that he could do anything he set his mind to. If you were in his presence, you also felt capable.

The whole time the mechanic was working on the airplane, my dad was having a Phil Attack. At one point, the mechanic tried to calm him down by saying that the Cub wasn't hurt that badly, and in his opinion, it could have been a lot worse. I agreed with that assessment and secretly gave Joe the credit. Finally, we got the new prop on and the landing gear repaired. I completed my duct-taping assignment while my dad spit words of wisdom at my neck. Still frothing at the mouth and flicking his false teeth, my dad flew the plane from the tundra back to the airport, where proper repairs could be accomplished. Because of his weight, he flew the Cub from the back seat, whereas I flew from the front.

It was at least two months before I got my airplane back that time. While I was waiting for my Cub to be repaired, I would ride with some of the pilots who were the first ones my dad hired when he started Yute Air Alaska. Two of the pilots were Yupik Eskimos from nearby villages. In those days, the only navigational tools were dead reckoning. No one knew the landscape better than them. I loved flying with them because they would teach me so much about the local area. There were hundreds of tricks associated with getting around in bad weather, and no one knew them better.

You often hear experienced pilots say things like, "You must know every bush and tree to survive." This is just an exaggeration;

don't take it literally. The only landmarks you need to know extremely well are things that identify entrances to passes, or things you can get headings from that will take you where you want to go. It doesn't hurt to learn basic tree and brush lines that are useful in identifying general areas. More often than not, these basic lines will assist you in finding an entrance to a pass.

I was taught to get around Bristol Bay a lot like an old blind dog gets around its yard. An old dog will walk along a familiar trail until it identifies a particular spot before heading off in some other direction. If you hang around the same yard long enough to learn every bush and stump, good for you, but you only need to know the basics to safely get around.

Before GPS, we used to keep a notebook in our pocket that had headings from different landmarks that we could review prior to the flight if need be. I'm grateful for the men who I idolized growing up for taking me under their wing and showing me the ropes. I'm also grateful for my guardian angel Joe who undoubtedly got the short straw when he was assigned my watch.

Chapter 9

SPENDING CHRISTMAS WITH JOE

One Christmas Eve, one of the company pilots was coming back from Togiak with a load of people in a Piper PA-32-300 Cherokee Six. The Cherokee Six was a low-wing 300-horsepower workhorse. It was about twenty-eight feet long and had a wingspan of thirty-three feet. It weighed about 1,800 pounds empty and cruised at nearly 170 miles per hour. The pilot was flying back using a route called the mail trail—nicknamed that because it was the most direct and commonly used pass through the mountains for small airplanes carrying the mail. The ceiling was low, and so was the visibility.

About halfway between Togiak and Dillingham there is a large lake named Ualik. Ualik Lake is north of the mail trail. Normally no one would have any reason to fly over Ualik Lake, but it was a lower route used when Summit Pass was not flyable. Summit Pass lay toward the east end of the mail trail and was at least two hundred feet higher than the other terrain at the east end of the pass.

The way I heard the story, the pilot was not able to get up into Summit Pass, so he started flying up the lake. About halfway up the lake, he flew right into the frozen snow-covered ice. The snow was only about a foot deep on the lake, and after the initial impact, the pilot simply pulled back the power and the plane came to a stop. There was no damage to the airplane or injuries to the passengers.

The pilot was not willing to risk taking off from the lake, even after the weather raised a bit. He wisely decided to leave the Cherokee sitting out on the ice and call for help. The only hope they had for getting off the lake that night was to keep the engine running and use the radio to try to contact one of the other company planes that might be flying the pass.

In those days, radios hadn't really caught on as far as using them to avoid other traffic, but they had proven useful in getting messages from airplane to airplane for dispatch purposes. Therefore, all Phil's company airplanes were on a company frequency. Just about two hours before dark, the pilot was able to talk to another aircraft coming back from ferrying reindeer meat between Hagemeister Island and Togiak. Hagemeister Island was about twenty-eight miles to the southwest of Togiak Village and was roughly twenty miles long and seven miles wide. At the time, Hagemeister Island had a large herd of reindeer living on it under the management of some reindeer herders who lived in Togiak Village.

The pilot coming to the rescue was flying a Cessna 185 Skywagon on wheel skis. The Cessna 185 is a six-seat, single-engine high-wing aircraft with non-retractable conventional landing gear and a tail wheel. It was approximately twenty-five feet long with a wingspan of thirty-five feet. It had a 300-horsepower engine and cruised at 145 miles per hour. This pilot landed beside the Cherokee and managed to cram all six passengers and the pilot into the smaller five-passenger airplane.

Of course, the whole situation caused a Phil Attack, but the next day, on our Lord Jesus's birthday, the weather had cleared and my dad was back to his old self. One thing about dad's attacks was that they didn't last very long, and when they were over, they were over. That Christmas morning, my dad and I jumped into the Cessna 185 and flew out to the lake. I assumed we were doing this so my dad could satisfy his curiosity. No matter what his reasons were, I was totally on board. I was thinking "road trip."

We looked over the airplane and couldn't find any signs of damage. The airplane simply landed on the lake in cruise power. My dad started scouting out the area, trying to find the best place for the Cherokee to take off. We soon found a windblown spot on the ice that was big enough to use as a runway. To get the airplane over to the location, we would have to taxi through some sizable snowdrifts.

At my age, I didn't weigh much, but my dad felt that me stretched out on the stabilator would be enough to keep the prop out of the drifts. A stabilator is like a horizontal stabilizer. They both provide longitudinal stability, but one is fixed at the rear of the aircraft with hinged elevators on the trailing edge of the stabilizer. The stabilator itself is fully movable, basically doing the job of both stabilizer and elevator. I don't think it matters which one it is when you're on top of it preparing yourself for a good ice-blasting.

I never questioned any of my dad's methods, and this time was no exception. I pulled my hat over my head, zipped up my jacket, and like the obedient son that I was, I lay down across the stabilator like I was waiting to be sacrificed. It wasn't long before I was being ice-blasted by all three hundred horses, and my dad wasn't holding any of them back. I guess he figured once he got moving, it really didn't matter whether or not I stayed on. Not wanting to disappoint my dad, I managed to cling to the stabilator like I was glued.

When we reached the bare spot, my dad just set the brakes

and jumped out. I was still collecting myself and shaking all the impacted snow and ice off my clothes. He never gave me any advice or direction of any kind other than, "Get in. I'll see you back in town." I had flown the airplane before from the left seat with my dad in the right seat, but this was going to be my first time flying that aircraft alone.

With the cold temperatures and just me in the airplane with hardly any gas, I never used a fraction of that bare spot for takeoff. The plane jumped off the ground and started heading for the sky like a homesick angel. I figured, *Hey, if I'm going to do this, let's make the best of it.*

I pushed that nose over, got back down to my J-3 cruising altitude of 150 feet, and put the engine in high cruise. I bogeyed through Summit Pass like I had always imagined myself doing. From that moment on, I was in love with Cherokees. I just liked the feel of the airplane. I was hoping Joe was enjoying the flight as much as I was because for once, he could just sit there with me and relax.

Chapter 10

IGNORING JOE'S LESSONS

I finally told my parents about my near-death experience while fishing in my little wooden boat, and they convinced me that it was time to buy an aluminum thirty-two-foot-long commercial fishing vessel and start fishing the bays I had grown up fishing with my dad and uncles. My parents helped me purchase the boat by cosigning a loan.

That summer, I signed on with Quean Fisheries, a cannery that was located up a muddy slough that dumped into Nushagak Bay about six miles south of Nushagak Point Beach. The cannery had its own short dirt runway that was in a half-moon shape around its large generator building. There wasn't any gravel around, so the airport was constructed of sand and dirt. In early spring and in heavy rains, the airport would get muddy, with large ruts. There were two large dirt waves at the south end. The only means of maintaining the runway was to drag a large metal screen behind a farm tractor.

I had landed on the runway hundreds of times with my Cub, primarily because it wasn't very busy and only about ten miles from Dillingham. During the summer, Yute Air would support the cannery by providing air transportation, including flying fish eggs back to Dillingham, where they could be flown out of town on larger aircraft like the Douglas DC-6.

The DC-6 is a four-engine piston-powered airliner built by Douglas Aircraft Company with the intent that it would serve as a transport aircraft for the military—and serve it did. However, after World War II, it was reworked to compete in the long-range commercial market. Many of these magnificent airplanes made their way to Alaska, where they are still in operation today serving the needs of rural communities. The DC-6 is about 106 feet long, with a wingspan of roughly 118 feet. Each of the four engines produces 2,400 horsepower. The DC-6 could leave Dillingham carrying about 28,000 pounds of whatever needed to be moved and would move it at about 315 miles per hour.

I wanted in the worst way to ride along on one of the flights that were transporting fish eggs from the Quean cannery to Dillingham, but eggs were hauled in the summer, and summer was a busy time for me as a commercial fisherman. Even when I was at the cannery waiting for another commercial opening, called a fishing period, I wasn't able to leave, because it was possible that what was known as an "emergency opening" would come with little warning.

I was also afraid to leave my boat tied up to the dock or tied to another boat in a boat raft when the tide was in because someone was always trying to leave or jockey for position alongside the dock during this period of time. If you were the boat that was tied alongside the dock, everyone depended on you to stay attached and not get hung up on a piling as the twenty-foot tide came rushing in or out. When the tide was out, all but the boats that were in the middle of the slew would go dry. The only time I felt comfortable leaving my boat alone was while my boat was dry or stuck in the middle of a boat raft that I knew wasn't going anywhere, and then I would only leave long enough to go to the airport and watch airplanes take off and land.

The primary airplane used in transporting the fish eggs was the Cessna 206. Between periods, if I wasn't jockeying boats, I would hang out at the airport and watch the airplanes launch into the air with full loads of eggs. The most effective direction for takeoff was toward the south to take advantage of the two large waves at the end of the dirt strip. The airplanes would launch into the air and hang inches above the grass in ground effect. There was always a competition between pilots to see who could take off with the largest number of boxes.

I got a kick out of standing around the airport watching the airplanes launch. There was always enough activity to keep me entertained, especially when someone not familiar with the airport would try to land from the south and launch off one of the waves at the end. There was a tall wind sock opposite the generator building that you had to miss in order to go around and try again. Crosswinds were also fun to watch: you never knew when someone was going to make some hair-raising move.

One day, I was hanging around the airport waiting for the next commercial fishing period when I heard a Cessna 180 starting its engine near the north end. The Cessna 180 is a smaller version of the Cessna 185. Suspecting it was someone I knew, I headed toward the north end of the runway around the back side of the generator building. As I was walking, I heard another airplane start up near the south end. I turned around and started running back. As I rounded the corner of the building, I could see the other airplane was just about in position to take off to the north. The airplanes were not able to see one another because of the generator building.

I continued to run toward the airplane in hopes of preventing it from moving. I got the pilot's attention and ran up to the airplane. The pilot opened his door, and I stood behind it holding it open against the propeller blast. As I was telling him why I had stopped him, the Cessna 180 came around the corner, tail high in the air. I think the 180 was light and could see what was going on as he rounded the corner because he lifted off and turned without even coming close to us. The radio, still not yet widely used to announce one's intentions, would have come in handy.

Despite the efforts of new pilots coming to Bristol Bay from various parts of the lower 48, the old-timers refused to use their radios except occasionally to come and go from Dillingham if the airplane was equipped. If one of the old-timers was approached about using the radio because of some mishap in the traffic pattern or near miss through a mountain pass, the response was normally, "Take your head out of the cockpit and look outside," or some variation of that. Potentially dangerous situations frequently arose because of the lack of communication.

New pilots to the area regularly used the radio between themselves. I think Joe intentionally brought me into this situation to teach me the importance of using the radio, but sadly, once again I ignored the sign he put directly in my face. Joe was always drawing my attention to lessons that would be in my best interest to learn, but I was so hung up on being what I perceived a bush pilot to be that I often misread the signs or ignored them all together.

Chapter 11

EVERYONE HAS A GUARDIAN ANGEL

One day, between periods, I was sitting on the grass at the south end of the Quean Fisheries cannery runway near a small parking area just large enough to park two airplanes. As I was sitting there, I heard what sounded like a hard landing by a Cherokee Six, a very distinct sound and a not uncommon one on that particular runway. I just sat there and waited to see who it was.

What I saw was quite alarming. One of my dad's new pilots who I had never met came taxiing around the generator building. The pilot was using an excessive amount of power, and it looked like his rear struts were flat. A second glance revealed that the main gear was missing. It took an enormous amount of power to get the airplane to the parking area, but to my astonishment, he actually pulled it off.

I was up on my feet by then and approaching the rear of the Cherokee when the right cockpit door opened and the pilot stepped out. The Cherokee features a large double door in the back on the left side for easy loading of passengers and cargo. There isn't a cockpit door on the left for the pilot—rather a door on the right side of the cockpit that leads onto the wing, with nonskid paint for safer walking that leads down along the fuselage and across the flap, where it ends. There is a step about six inches lower than the flap that bridges the gap between the flap and the ground.

The pilot who stepped out looked like something right out of a pilot magazine: slicked-back hair, sunglasses, nice shirt, leather jacket, khakis, and shiny black shoes. This guy looked like a pilot; he was even holding a clipboard in his right hand. The only thing missing was the scarf. Honestly, I had never seen a person dress like that except in pilot magazines.

He stepped off the wing, chest all puffed out, smiling from ear to ear. He had landed at the area's most difficult airport. The runway was more than a little intimidating if you hadn't ever landed there before. It didn't hit him that something might be wrong until he stepped off the wing onto the ground, which was literally one inch lower than the flap. His facial expression soon turned from a smile to one of bewilderment, and he stumbled for his footing after expecting more of a drop.

I didn't know what to say, I just stood there looking at the pilot wondering to myself, who is this guy? I must admit, I was admiring the way he was dressed; however, I'm not sure how practical the outfit was for the job he was doing. I don't know how he taxied with missing landing gear. Frankly, if I hadn't seen it for myself, I certainly wouldn't have believed it.

Without saying a word, I started following the trail that the belly of the Cherokee had left behind. It wasn't until I reach the north end of the runway that I could see the two main gears still firmly planted in the two-foot-deep drainage ditch at the end of the airport. The pilot apparently possessed the skills to dress himself like a pilot, but he wasn't skilled enough to be land at the cannery. He had absolutely no idea that the impact he had undoubtedly felt had left his main gear back in the ditch.

I walked back to where the airplane was parked. The pilot was still there walking around the plane, performing what looked like a preflight. I told him not to feel bad; this kind of thing happens. The truth is, my dad probably took this guy out for three or four touch-and-goes and then turned him loose. Right after that, our dispatcher probably handed him a clipboard with a list of names on it and told him to go to the cannery and pick the people up. If he had gotten any advice on how to get in or out of that runway, it was probably penciled out on a piece of paper towel that was lying on the counter. I had been around my dad long enough to know that no matter how this man had ended up in his particular situation, my dad was at least partially to blame. I guarantee the man hadn't received any more than the bare-minimum training.

The pilot eventually told me his name, and I took him up to the pay phone where he made the dreaded call. It wasn't long before my dad showed up with two mechanics, so I decided to retreat to my boat, electing to miss out on all the drama associated with this type of ordeal. I know the man had a guardian angel of his own, and Joe was probably welcoming that angel to Bristol Bay and letting him know that this was only the beginning.

Chapter 12

A FROSTY LESSON WITH JOE AT MY SIDE

The summer I turned seventeen, I planned to spend the winter with my uncle in Walla Walla, Washington. I was going to attend school at Walla Walla Valley Seventh-Day Adventist Academy and take flying lessons at a nearby airport. I did more getting into trouble than flying, and eventually I got out of control to the point that my uncle sent me back home to Alaska. At least I had paid enough attention to have completed all the necessary training required to get a private license before being sent home.

My dad was a designated examiner for Bristol Bay, and I managed to pull myself together enough for him to give me my private license sometime during the winter. Once I had my private license, I was allowed to fly the Cessna 206 and Cherokee Six. I was given permission to fly those airplanes in local area and traffic patterns as much as I wanted to build time for my commercial license when I turned eighteen.

Early one morning, I decided to fly a Cherokee that had been sitting out all night and had heavy frost on the wings, stabilizers, and control surfaces. I had flown Cherokees with frost before, but this was just a little more than I had ever flown with. I decided to fly the frost off the airframe rather than sweep it off or pull the plane into the hangar. Looking back, I think it was more of a young man's experiment than a sound decision.

I taxied back to use runway 19 for departure, even though it was slightly uphill for a good portion of the runway. This way I was heading out toward the bay, not toward the trees. The airplane took off just like I expected it to. Once airborne, however, I realized it was taking nearly full right ailerons deflection to maintain level flight. I was confident this was only a temporary condition, so I elected to continue out over the bay in hopes that the warm air would get rid of the frost for me.

I cleared the end of the runway and descended down to just feet over the water. I was still holding nearly full aileron deflection and was starting to second-guess my decision. After one or two long minutes flying feet over the water, I started trying to think up an exit strategy. I figured with minimal turning, I could align myself with the old Clark's Point runway, which was only feet above sea level. After sufficient time had passed to reacquaint myself with prayer, I managed to maneuver myself over against the western shoreline and was beginning a gentle left turn to attempt to line up with the Clark's Point runway.

About then, my brilliant plan to fly the frost off rather than use a broom or push the airplane into the hangar finally started working. I kept the gentle turn going and got the airplane heading back toward Dillingham. I stayed as low as I could for another couple of minutes and by then had gained complete control over the aircraft. I climbed up to about 900 feet, joined the Dillingham traffic pattern, and continued shooting touch-and-goes for about an hour before calling it quits. I wish I could say that I never flew with frost on my wings again, but sadly, it was going to take more than that to wise me up.

I later reflected on what had happened and couldn't help but remember all the stupid stunts I had pulled over the years, and not just in airplanes. I began to recall that every time I would get myself in a jam, Joe was there to comfort me and get me out of my situation. I closed my eyes and took the time to thank God for assigning Joe as my guardian angel. I then took a minute to speak to Joe.

I hadn't spoken to Joe for a while, and I felt guilty about that. I made a new promise to communicate more, even when I wasn't asking for a miracle. When I spoke to Joe, I always spoke to him out loud, like he was right beside me. Everyone has a guardian angel, and I am grateful that Joe was assigned to me.

Chapter 13

ANGELS DON'T JUDGE US

In September, after another great fishing season, I was approached by a friend who wanted to go moose hunting. I didn't want to go, because the one time I had gone moose hunting, I ended up packing moose for what seemed like days and hated every minute of it. I hadn't considered ever going again.

My dad didn't do much hunting, but he had been doing all the flying for Togiak cannery for several years, and to thank them for all the business, he offered to take the chefs and culinary staff on a moose hunt. Togiak Fisheries is located on the east side of the north end of Togiak Bay, only about two miles from the village of Togiak. Really, he was sucking up to the chefs because they always fed his pilots whenever they stopped by the dining hall. It didn't matter whether it was mealtime or not; the kitchen was always open to my dad's pilots. My dad appreciated that immensely and wanted to pay them back for all their generosity.

Nine hunters, including my dad and my uncle and not counting me, ended up going. My dad and uncle both had airplanes and transported us all to a little airport a hundred miles southeast of Dillingham called Fort Jensen. Fort Jensen airport is east of the line between Egegik Bay and Ugashik Bay, and about ten miles from the coast.

When we arrived, we flew around the area looking for moose and spotted nine all in one tight group. They looked to be all bulls. I don't remember whether or not it was legal to fly and hunt on the same day, but I do know my dad rallied the troops and off we went after the nine moose. At some point, we all spread out, and I hung with my dad. We lost track of everyone else and were just heading in the general direction of the moose on our own.

We must have all popped out into the clearing that all the moose were in at the same time as everyone else because the moment we saw all nine moose, gunshots rang out from every direction. Once the shooting started, my dad raised his gun and shot the closest one to him. There were moose staggering and falling all around us.

When the shooting stopped, I could see someone in the middle of all the dead moose with a white T-shirt on the top of his gun barrel. He was waving it in the air like he was surrendering to the enemy. As it turned out, there were eight bull moose and what appeared to be one lucky cow. However, there was a cook standing there with his gun pointed at the sole survivor. I remember everyone hollering at him not to shoot, but seconds later, a shot rang out, and the cow was dead. Our moose was still alive, so my dad tried to hand me his pistol to end its suffering, but I had never killed anything before, and although I wasn't against it and certainly didn't like seeing the animal suffer, I refused. So my dad put the moose out of its misery himself.

After all the excitement was over, there was a quick roll call to make sure everyone was okay. Then the knives came out, and the hair started to fly. The next thing I knew, I had an old metal pack frame on my back with a hind quarter strapped to it, and I was sent back to find the airplane. I've never been so scared in all my life. I was all alone in the brush with eighty pounds of bear bait on my back. If you think I wasn't talking to God going down that narrow path, you'd be wrong.

After stumbling down the trail thinking of all the things I still wanted to accomplish in my life, I found the airplane and unstrapped the bear bait from my back. After I caught my breath, I headed back for another load. I remember making trip after trip back to the airfield with loads of bloody meat.

My dad and uncle started hauling the meat back to Dillingham as soon as the first load was staged. They arrived back at Fort Jensen before dark and help set up camp. I worked up quite an appetite packing meat. I wasn't much of a meat-eater, but I think I can safely say in all my years living in Alaska, that was the only time I truly enjoyed eating moose meat.

The only reason I was considering another moose hunting trip was because on this trip, I was going to be the pilot, not the bear-bait transporter. I said yes, and we loaded up Little Yeller and flew up the Nushagak River looking for moose. We ended up flying about forty-five river miles before we found a spot with plenty of moose.

We didn't really want to camp right on a bear trail, so we found an island to camp on. The island had a clearing on one side that looked long enough to get the Cub in and out comfortably. The landing zone was full of tall grass. As it turned out, the grass was hiding lots of driftwood, brush, and uneven ground that we bounced over, but we came to a stop without tipping over. No problem, we thought—we would clean up the landing zone in the morning.

Some friends of mine had seen my Cub and stopped by to visit. They were concerned that they hadn't got their meat for the winter and asked if I would use the Cub to find them some moose. The deal was that if I could spot them a moose with the

Cub, they would shoot, butcher, and haul it back to where we could come and pick up our share. This sounded like a great deal for me. I wasn't a vegetarian, but I hadn't been raised eating meat, and when I did it was usually chicken or fish. I hadn't developed a taste for wild game. My friend, on the other hand, had his heart set on shooting his own moose. I convinced him that this was only our backup plan, and I would spot him a moose.

The next morning, we all got busy clearing driftwood and brush out of the way so we would have a better landing area. The clearing I picked out had trees on one end, so it was one way in and one way out. I used a shiny new tin can from the previous evening's supper to mark where I was to touch down on our landing area when we got back for the night. The strip of ground that we cleared wasn't much wider than the cub, and lining up on the tin can was going to be critical. We soon took to the air and began looking for moose.

There wasn't a big presence of fish and game officers in the area we were in because most of the land along the river belonged to the native corporation, and no one hunted there except locals. We didn't have a radio for communications, so the signal for the guys in the boat was for me to first buzz the moose, then fly over the boat, and finally head straight for where the moose was hiding and wiggle my wings from side to side. A buzz is just a fancy word for descending sharply over the object of interest and then climbing out rapidly, drawing attention to oneself for any number of reasons.

We soon found two moose close to the river in a small clearing. I made an obvious buzz over the moose and headed straight for the boat. I buzzed the boat for fun and then went back around, flew over them again, and headed straight for the moose. When directly over the moose, I wiggled my wings from side to side. We then headed off to find more moose.

We soon found two large bulls in a dried-up creek bed that was about sixty feet wide. Excited about our new discovery, we flew back to check on the hunters who had gone into the woods after the two moose. They had already shot and killed both moose and were beginning to butcher them up. They waved frantically at us out of excitement.

I needed to get their attention before the moose wandered off. The moose were in a great location, and I really wanted at least two of the men to break off and take the skiff over and drop the two moose. I didn't know if they understood what I was trying to say or if they just thought I was being an annoying jerk. I was buzzing, wiggling my wings side to side, doing whatever I could to get them to follow me. They just kept cutting up meat and hauling it out to the skiff.

My friend finally came up with the solution. He suggested that we fly over the moose and shoot them ourselves from the airplane. I really didn't like the idea, but it did present some new challenges for me as a pilot, and I started to warm up to the suggestion. I flew over to the area where the moose were and began forming a plan. My friend had a high powered rifle with a scope. I tried to convince him to take the scope off because in the plan I was developing, he wouldn't need it. I was also afraid that with the barrel being four inches lower than the scope, he might accidentally shoot our strut. A strut is a brace that quite literally holds the wing in place.

My friend refused to take the scope off, but he did promise not to look through it. He was an airplane mechanic and knew how important the strut was to us. I soon agreed that the scope could stay on. The plan that I came up with was to slip the Cub down into the dried-up creek bed right on top of the moose. The door of the Cub would be open, and my friend would have a large area to shoot out of. It would be noisy to fly with the door open, but we could still communicate by yelling at each other.

I had been flying the Cub by myself for a while now, and I was beginning to get very comfortable. The J-3 was designed to be flown from the rear seat when by yourself because of weight distribution, but I had always flown it from the front, even by myself, because of my size.

Over the years, I'd perfected the slip and felt very confident that I could slip down between the trees, fly over the creek bed, and end up within ten feet above the moose. From over the moose, as long as I didn't advance the throttle too quickly, I should be able to make a nice smooth getaway. With the gunner ready and the moose still standing in the creek bed, I lined up, pulled on the carburetor heat, and began my slip. The Cub dropped perfectly over the moose. The moose wasn't fifteen feet away from the door opening when I heard the shot.

I begin to advance the throttle slowly, gently started releasing the rudder, and flew out above the trees just as I had planned. I hollered back at my friend, "Did you get it?"

My friend hollered back, "I don't know. All I seen was his hair in the scope."

That wasn't what I wanted to hear, so I snapped my head over my shoulder to look at our strut. I couldn't see any damage, and I was relieved.

As I turned back around and spotted our moose, I was horrified to find that my friend had blown its jawbone off, and the poor moose was running down the creek bed. I panicked, never wanting to see an animal suffer. I yanked on the carburetor heat and immediately started a slip down onto the moose while yelling at my friend take another shot. I got down within ten feet this time and gently started my escape as I heard the gunshot. I quickly got the airplane turned back around as soon as I could, and this time the moose was lying down. There was still one more moose, but after seeing the last moose suffer, I couldn't allow any more shooting out of the airplane. Pumped up on adrenaline, I started heading for the location where we had left the hunters. En route, I started to relax a little and looked over the area outside the door.

I noticed a small, round, clean spot on the upper part of my tundra tire. I yelled back at my friend and asked him if he had shot our tire. He answered no, but not believing him, I told him to poke the tire with the rifle. He poked the tire, and as I feared, the tire was flat. Now I was in a pickle. I could try to get the hunters' attention and get them over to the moose, but if they didn't get the message in time, I wouldn't have enough daylight left to get to Dillingham, fix the tire, and get back to my landing location. Figuring worst-case scenario the moose would be okay until morning, I decided to make a quick pass over the hunters to attempt to lead them to the moose before proceeding on to Dillingham.

As I approached their location, I could see that they had already gotten all the meat to the thirty-two-foot powerboat, and the skiff was already heading in our direction. Finally, something was going right. I buzzed over the skiff, turned back around, flew back over the skiff, and headed toward the dead moose. As I approached the moose, I dove down, wiggling my wings from side to side, and then I headed for Dillingham. When we got to Dillingham, I landed right in front of the hangar on the ramp instead of the runway because I didn't want to take the extra time to limp into parking with a flat tire. This drew more attention than I wanted.

Unfortunately, when the bullet exited the tire, it blew a major hole—way bigger than the tiny little clean spot the entry had made. The damage was too severe to patch. I went to the house of the only person I knew who would possibly have a spare tire that I could borrow. The man no longer had a J-3, but over the years he had owned several of them. He not only had a spare tire, but it was mounted on a wheel exactly like mine and was greased and ready to go. I didn't get into much detail with him, but he had been a neighbor of ours my whole life, so he pretty much knew I was up to something.

I rushed back to the airport as fast as I could, and we quickly put the tire on the Cub. My friend said he had been trying to avoid answering too many questions. He had made up some excuse about a piece of driftwood popping our tire. He also said that my dad had dropped by but hadn't said much. My friend indicated that my dad just shook his head and walked away.

We got the tire on and everything seemed to be in order, so we took back off for our campsite. When we reach the campsite, it was starting to get dark. I made several attempts to line up with the tin can, but every time I would spot the can, it would be off to one side or another. I soon became desperate. Running out of daylight, I started to panic a little inside.

After about four attempts, it was really starting to get dark. I finally hit the mark, and the can appeared right in front of me. I chopped the power and tried to pull back on the stick. It wouldn't budge. I pushed it forward slightly and tried to pull it back again. It still wouldn't budge. Now it was pushed forward even farther. We were on the ground by now, and the tail was high in the air. There wasn't much I could do except go along for the ride.

I pulled the throttle off and held the stick back the best I could. I said a quick prayer as I bounced over the uneven terrain. Going around for another try was out of the question now that my controls were locked. I wasn't perfectly lined up with our runway, and I plowed through the sticks and the moguls I was trying to avoid. The prop was cutting through the grass, and the tires were throwing sticks up in the air as we bounced alongside the intended runway.

I don't know how we kept from tipping over, although I'm sure Joe and my friend's angel could tell you. We jumped out to try to figure out what had happened. My friend quickly spotted the problem and pulled a large caliber bullet casing from inside the hole where the control stick is normally mounted.

I had removed the control stick before we started our adventure to give my friend more room. Normally there is a cover that goes over the hole when you remove the stick, but I had no such cover. I guess if the bullet was going to jam up our controls, it couldn't have happened at a better time, even though we nearly crashed. Feeling blessed to be on the ground safe and that we had pulled off a successful day, we found somewhere to tie the Cub down for the night.

In the morning, my friends dropped by and told us that they had found the moose we had shot and had even found the other moose that was in the same general area. They said they had enough moose to tide them over until the December hunt and were heading home. They told my hunting partner that one of the moose had a sixty-plus-inch rack, and they didn't have any use for it. They said that they had kept it just in case he wanted it. He told them that he was grateful that they had been thinking of him, and he would pick up the moose rack with the meat. After my friends left, we discussed going home ourselves.

That was most definitely the last time I have ever let anyone shoot a rifle from the back seat of my Cub. When I finally made it home, I knew exactly who I wanted to thank for keeping us safe once again. The experience reinforced my theory that Joe played a much bigger part in my life than I ever imagined. That night, when I was alone, I spoke to Joe and thanked him for always being there for me and promised once again that I would be more careful so that he wouldn't have to work so hard.

I believe angels know all the great things that make us who we are. I believe angels are there on the darkest and coldest of nights. I believe angels don't judge us, they don't tire of helping us, and they don't interfere with what we are doing. They are simply by our side to assist in any way they can. I believe that if you ever get to feeling lonely or scared, just talk to your angel. He'll be right by your side. I believe we are never truly alone.

After that trip, I left for Yuma, Arizona, where I had planned to get a commercial and instrument rating while staying with my grandparents. I was starting my career in aviation in a bit of a quandary. I wanted in the worst way to follow the example of the experienced bush pilots in the area, and on the other hand I felt some alliance with the new pilots coming into the area who were bringing change along with them.

I had experienced what I thought was real bush flying, but looking back, I can only conclude that my perception of the bush pilot was nothing more than a teenage boy living out some fantasy. I had made up my mind to purchase and use a radio, and for this I am grateful. But it wouldn't be until later in life that I truly joined the alliance to help tame Bristol Bay.

Chapter 14

LEARNING MORALS FROM JOE

The year 1979 was a great one for commercial fishing. I had made enough money to fly down to Yuma, Arizona, and spend three months living with my grandparents and getting my commercial and instrument rating. I borrowed a three-wheeled bicycle from my grandparents that hadn't been used in quite some time; after some attention, the bike was as good as new. The bicycle had a large rack on the back for carrying groceries and supplies. It wasn't the style of bike the other eighteen-year-olds were riding, but it worked for what I needed it for.

When I arrived at the flight school I discovered that Yuma had two parallel runways. One was strictly military and the other strictly civilian. I found it fascinating to watch the military planes come and go.

Shortly after my arrival, there was an air show. I had never been to an air show before, so I was eager to attend. There were hundreds of airplanes, and I could look inside military aircraft I hadn't even heard about. The airplane that particularly fascinated me was the Harrier jet. The Harrier jet, informally referred to as the Harrier Jump Jet, is a family of jet-powered attack aircraft capable of vertical/short takeoff and landing operations.

The military put on a demonstration with the Harrier jet that completely blew my mind.

I had seen the F-16 Fighting Falcon, a single-engine supersonic fighter with a distinct frameless bubble canopy. The F-16 was forty-nine feet long and had a wingspan of thirty-two feet. Three of the villages near Dillingham were within a military operations area for a nearby air force base located at King Salmon, Alaska. Occasionally we would see F-16s flying by. In fact, I had even experienced the speed of sound for the first time at Ekwok, Alaska—the oldest continuously occupied Yupik village on the Nushagak River. Ekwok is forty-three miles northeast of Dillingham.

I was standing on the side of Ekwok Airport one morning while on a ride-along with one of Yute Air's pilots when I saw an F-16 streak by. The jet was just off to the side of the airport and only three hundred feet up. I observed what looked like an explosion come out the back end of the jet as it zipped by. After the explosion, it shot off like a rocket.

While this was happening, I was just starting to hear the jet arrive. Just when it sounded like it was right next to me, I heard a window-shattering explosion. Soon, another F-16 showed up. He did the same exact thing. The F-16s were so close you could see the pilots waving at us from the bubble canopy just before they hit their afterburners.

I got serious about my training and soon discovered that not too far outside of Yuma there was an abandoned airport. I'm not sure why the airport was there, but it was pretty nice compared to the airports I was used to. During my training, I would leave Yuma and fly up over this abandoned airport and do maneuvers. I would land occasionally to eat my sack lunch or just walk around and stretch my legs. This airport was out in the middle of nowhere; there wasn't anything around for miles.

One day, I was flying over the abandoned airport and needed to land and stretch my legs. As I landed, the right tire of the Piper PA-28 Cherokee 140 I was flying popped. The Cherokee 140 was smaller than the Piper PA-32 Cherokee Six 300 my dad let me fly off the frozen lake. The Cherokee 140 was designed for flight training and only had a 140-horsepower engine compared to the 300-horsepower Cherokee Six.

I hardly noticed the tire blowing upon landing because of the wide wheelbase. It pulled slightly to the right, and I could tell something was wrong, but it sure didn't pull like Little Yeller did when I blew her tire. I jumped out to inspect the damage, and sure enough, the tire was flat. I was a lot like my dad when it came to sitting around, so I decided to do something even if it turned out to be wrong. I decided that it was in my best interest to take off on the flat tire and fly back to Yuma.

By now, it had become routine for me to ask God for help, especially when I was blatantly doing something questionable. It was comforting to know that I could always count on Joe to be right there with me, no mater what.

The military airport had been shut down for several days after the air show. The civilian airport was still open, and the tower for both runways was operated by the military. I took off with the flat tire without any difficulty and called the tower from about ten miles away. I told them that I had felt something on takeoff, and I suspected it might be one of my tires. The military was used to dealing with student pilots, so they were very accommodating. The tower suggested I fly by close to the tower so they could inspect for damage. I was more than willing to accommodate, knowing full well that if the tire was still there, they would see a normal-looking tire like the one I had seen after Little Yeller's tire was shot.

I slowed down and flew by the tower window as requested.

As I suspected, they couldn't see anything wrong but decided to take advantage of the opportunity and use it as a training exercise. They told me to land on the military side and directed me to circle just off the end of the military airport. Within minutes, they had the emergency equipment in place. They had no less than six big fire trucks stretched out along the airport, jeeps filled with military personnel, and ambulances coming out of the woodwork. It was quite a reception.

Once everyone was in place, they instructed me to land and remain inside the aircraft until the responders opened my door. I landed, and as I anticipated, it was uneventful. I stopped in the middle of the runway and shut the engine off, and within seconds military personnel were all around the airplane. Men in firefighting suits rushed up to the door. The men looked more like they were responding to a biohazard than a fire, but they whisked me away from the aircraft with speed and precision. When we were a safe distance away, the men took off their masks. They shook my hand and told me that was the most fun they'd had in a long time.

It was quite a welcome to Yuma. They called the owner of the company—a first for me. I was usually the one making the call. Maintenance came over in a vehicle prepared to tow the crippled airplane back to the flight school. The military told them they were welcome to fix the tire on the closed runway to minimize any further damage. The military put me in their jeep, and after I did some paperwork, they gave me a ride back to the flight school. The flight school had even more paperwork for me to do, but soon I was heading home for the day.

Early the next morning, I got checked out in one of the retractable-gear Piper PA-28R-180 Cherokee Arrow. It was a little bigger and faster than the Cherokee 140 and was a better aircraft for learning about high-altitude flying—something I knew nothing about. I started to plot a cross-country course to Flagstaff, Arizona. Flagstaff lies near the southwest edge of the Colorado Plateau and sits at about 7,000 feet up on a mountain. I had never been to Flagstaff, but I had heard other students talking about it and the challenges that high-altitude flying presented.

Wanting to see what it was all about, I set out on my adventure. It was a beautiful day, and I was flying a zigzag pattern across the desert, taking in all the sights. It wasn't long before I needed to stretch my legs—at least that's the excuse I gave myself for landing on a crop-dusting runway I happened to fly over.

Most of the airports the crop dusters operated from were private dirt landing strips that usually had at least one hangar for maintenance. Back then, the typical crop duster I saw flying around was a 600-horsepower radial-engine-powered Ayres S-2R Thrush. It was about twenty-nine feet long and had a wingspan of forty-four feet. It could carry about four hundred gallons of liquid. I landed and pulled into the parking spot in front of the hangar. The hangar door was open, and the mechanics were working on one of the crop dusters inside, out of the hot Arizona sun.

I was so excited to be on the same runway as crop dusters, I must have gone brain-dead for a minute because when I parked in front of the hangar, I filled it with dust. As I was ruining the day of about three people inside the hangar, I realized what I'd done, and I thought, *Oh my God, these guys are going to kill me. I know my dad's mechanics would have.*

I had two choices: one, I could shut the engine off and apologize; or two, I could fill the hangar up with even more dust and run. Feeling outnumbered, I took the coward's way out. I gave the hangar one more big blast of Arizona dust and immediately took off. After liftoff, I attempted to retract the landing gear, and as if I was being punished for my foolishness, my gear wouldn't retract. Apparently, Joe was teaching me a lesson in good morals and wanted me to return and apologize.

We often had differences of opinion about right and wrong. I knew when Joe thought I was doing wrong because he would find creative ways to point out my questionable decisions. In this case, I figured Joe to be wrong, but I knew that I wouldn't have enough gas to make it to my destination without lifting the gear, so I decided to land on the same runway and stay at the far end. I wanted to look at the landing gear to see if I could spot something obvious. It was a long runway, and I figured I would have enough time to make an escape if need be.

I landed at the far end of the dirt field and turned the airplane into position for takeoff. I jumped out and was looking for anything obviously wrong with the landing gear. While I was under the airplane, a crop duster took off. I didn't think much of it until he came roaring down the runway, missing my airplane by two feet at the most. I decided to make my escape, but as I crawled out from under the wing, I could see the crop duster climbing up at an impressive rate.

Out of curiosity, I just stood there looking up at the crop duster as it did some sort of wingover maneuver I had seen them do while dusting crops. Seconds later, it dawned on me to get back under the wing because an overwhelming amount of what I can only hope was water started coming out from underneath the wing of the crop duster. From under my wing, I could see not one truck but several trucks heading down the middle of the runway. It was now or never.

As I emerged from under the wing, I could see the crop duster winding up for another pass. I jumped in the cockpit and got the engine going. By now, it was obvious to me that I wasn't going to have enough runway to take off because of the approaching trucks. I did what any Alaska-raised boy would do: I shoved the throttle against the firewall and took a sharp left onto a road that cut between two fields. I forced the airplane into the air with an armload of flaps and never looked back.

I figure Joe felt it was best to let me leave after teaching me a valuable lesson about choices because the landing gear came up and away I went. I didn't waste any more time getting to Flagstaff. The landing was definitely different from what I was used to, but uneventful.

I went into one of the local establishments and had lunch. It was an extremely hot day, and my white Alaskan skin was starting to smolder, so I figured I better be getting back to my grandparents' air-conditioned house. Flagstaff Airport is at an elevation of 7,000 feet and is 8,800 feet long. I fueled up with gas and, having no formal high-altitude hot-weather training, positioned myself at the end of one of the runways.

I applied full throttle, and at first the only thing I could see moving was the indicator for the cylinder head temperature. The prop was making a funny noise, like cavitation on a boat. Finally, the plane started to creep along the runway. I could feel the prop starting to bite, and eventually the Cherokee started to fly. As soon as I could, I dropped down to an altitude I was more comfortable at.

I could have counted with just my fingers how many times I had been above 2,000 feet in a small plane. This was a unique experience for me, and in the end, I finally had to admit that Joe was right. At the same time, I was grateful not to be in a shallow Arizona grave in the back of some hangar. A short time later, I finished my ratings and headed back to Alaska.

Chapter 15

OVER THIRTY-FOOT SEAS WITH JOE AT MY SIDE

It was spring when I arrived back in Dillingham with my commercial and instrument rating in my hand. Anxious to get my career as a bush pilot started, I asked my dad if he would check me out in the Cherokee Six. I chose the Cherokee primarily because I fell in love with the airplane on Christmas Day taking off from that frozen lake. Within days, I got a check ride in the Cherokee and started to fly freight and passengers to and from the nearby villages.

All my life, I'd spent the summers on the water. With the snow nearly gone, I was starting to feel the powerful pull of the ocean. I got the urge to try my hand at commercial herring fishing in the Togiak district. I was somewhat familiar with the Togiak area, but herring fishing was totally new.

The less expensive way to get into herring fishing was to use a gill net because my boat was already set up for that type of fishing. All I had to do was purchase the nets, ropes, and anchors. There were boats the size of mine seining for herring, but the cost associated with going that route—for example, the modifications to the boat, seine skiff, seine net, and employing a spotter airplane—was more than I could afford.

As it turned out, I was right not to go too far into debt because my first year herring fishing was a complete disaster. I hired an inexperienced crew member, the kind affectionately called a greenhorn. Most herring gill-net fishermen had at least two crew members, but I was trying to save money, so I elected to fish with just the two of us.

It took us about two weeks to get the boat ready and outfitted for our adventure. The season started out with us anchored out along with thirty other boats in Kulukak Bay, about forty miles southwest of Dillingham. Kulukak Bay is the first bay west of Nushagak Bay, and it's the eastern border of the Togiak herring-fishery boundary. Until there is enough biomass to justify a commercial opening, fishermen must stand by at the ready. Once the announcement came over the VHF radio—a line-of-sight radio that Fish and Game used to make opening announcements from a nearby location—we began our new adventure. We found a semi-secluded area on the west side of Kulukak Bay about midway between the entrance of the bay and to the north end.

Herring fishing was different from gill-net fishing for salmon because the herring nets were anchored in three separate fifty-fathom sections rather than attached to a drifting boat. We watched our gear from a short distance away for a couple of hours before pulling one of the fifty fathom nets in. Another difference between gillnetting salmon and gillnetting herring is that you shake the herring out of the net by the hundreds rather then pick them out one at a time. After shaking all the fish out of the first net and shoveling them into the fish hold, we set it back out and moved on to the next net. It wasn't long before we had about 19,000 pounds of herring onboard the thirty-two-foot boat.

The wind was starting to pick up, and with 19,000 pounds of fish onboard, the boat was getting hard to handle. We pulled in the two nets that hadn't been out very long and elected to leave the net that was loaded with fish in the water—figuring it was better off in the water than taking a chance on overloading the boat. We had no choice but to abandon our gear and try to get the boat unloaded at the hundred-foot tender that was anchored at the entrance of the bay in deep water. The tender was set up to unload boats by the means of a large suction tube that they would lower into the boat for us to vacuum our herring up with.

As we left the protection of shallow water, we noticed that the waves had grown to a frightening size. We had a small eighteen-foot aluminum skiff that we were towing behind us that we were told would come in handy later when the spawn-on-kelp season started, but in these conditions, the boat was in our way. As we approached the tender, we could only see the small skiff as it came over the top of a wave while we were climbing the next one.

I had never experienced rough seas of this magnitude. The closest I had ever come to being this scared out on the ocean was when I was about nine years old. I was fishing with my dad, and we were repositioning the boat from Nushagak Bay to the Kvichak Bay.

Kvichak Bay is an arm on the northeast side of Bristol Bay in southern Alaska. The Kvichak River flows into the bay at its furthest northeast point. The Naknek River, another major river, comes in from the east about twenty miles to the south of the Kvichak. In terms of commercial fishing for salmon, Kvichak Bay has within it two fishing districts: Egegik and Naknek-Kvichak.

Dad and I were on our way to fish the Naknek-Kvichak district. As we ventured out past the protection of Nushagak Bay, we were exposed to much rougher seas for about thirty miles before entering the semi-protected waters of Kvichak Bay. It was in that thirty-mile stretch in my dad's thirty-foot wooden fishing boat that we began taking on water from the ocean spray splashing up from the bow that was cutting through the large waves.

I was told to use our bilge pump to keep our boat from sinking. Our bilge pump was just like the ones you see in old Western movies. The pump was mounted in the middle of the boat just behind the driving station. The boat had fish holds in the center section covered with plywood, so I wasn't in danger of falling into a fish hole, but the sides of the boat were without a railing. A person could easily fall overboard with one misstep.

The pump had a pipe that reached the lowest point in the haul. Above the deck was the body of the pump with a handle almost out of my reach, but on my tiptoes, I could hang on and bring it down as it pumped water from below. I liked to pump water out of the boat while in calm seas, but this was in rough seas, and I was scared for my life. I would shut my eyes whenever the cold spray hit my face, and I took advantage of each time I closed my eyes to pray for my life. I now know that Joe was standing behind me with his wings spread around me like a fence, protecting me from falling overboard.

The driving station was open in the back, and I remember pumping on the handle as hard as I could with tears running down my face. Whenever I would stop, my dad would just look at me and say, "You had better not stop pumping, or we are going to sink." Looking back as an adult, I don't think we were in danger of sinking as much as he didn't want the pump to lose prime in case he needed to step back and pump.

The pump was supposed to have a check valve built into it to keep it from losing its prime, but I think it was worn out because it would lose its prime if left alone for very long. I was trying to be brave and not let my dad know I was crying. The ocean spray was helping me camouflage my tears. My dad had to constantly steer the boat because we were being tossed about like a small bottle adrift at sea, so I stayed at the pump station for this section of the trip. Once we turned the corner and started heading into Kvichak Bay, the spray quit coming over the boat, and I could try my hand at steering while my dad pumped the boat out.

I was grown up now, in my boat full of herring, and although I was good at keeping the boat straight in rough seas, I could feel a knot developing in my throat. It would've been easy to start crying, but I was an adult with big-boy responsibilities. Knowing that I had Joe by my side was comforting, and I was confident he would do everything in his power to make sure we came out of this situation alive and possibly a little wiser.

Shrugging off the danger, I continued toward the tender. As I was carefully making my way over each thirty-foot-plus wave, trying desperately not to let the boat turn sideways as I surfed down the backside of each wave, I heard an announcement from the captain of the tender over the VHF radio warning all boats to stay away from his vessel because the waves were getting much too dangerous for anyone to get too close. I wasn't sure where to take the boat to hide from the storm. The closest place I was familiar with was twenty miles away, and I wasn't looking forward to traveling that far.

I was listening to the VHF radio in scan mode so I could hear every conversation in the area, hoping to hear a familiar voice. I began to hear other fishermen talking about a bay called Metervik. Metervik Bay was at the entrance of Kulukak Bay, tucked into the southwest corner.

You could only enter Metervik Bay with large boats on nearly high tide. The bay was rocky, but with little other protection for miles in either direction, no one had any choice but to get into the bay because the worst of the storm was yet to come. I ended up being the last boat to enter the bay, just as the tide was getting to the point where I would have been cut off from my lifeline and forced to travel twenty miles in worse conditions than I was in to seek other shelter. We set our anchor and pulled our small skiff alongside.

The bay itself, although protected from rough seas, didn't provide much shelter from the wind. The west end of the bay went completely dry, and when it did, many of the fishermen were tying their boats to nearby rocks. Where I went dry, there weren't any large rocks to tie onto. When the tide came back in, it was relatively calm in the bay, but the wind was over fifty miles an hour and our anchor wouldn't hold. Rather than sit and idle with the boat in gear to minimize dragging, I elected to let the anchor drag for a quarter mile or so and then pick it up, run back into the wind, and drop the anchor again.

I was reluctant to let my inexperienced deckhand stand watch. I eventually wore down though, and out of exhaustion let him monitor our situation—but I made him promise to wake me up before it was time to move again. It wasn't long before I was in a deep sleep.

On a boat, you learn to notice the subtlest change in the boat's behavior, but in this case the boat behaved the same until it hit the beach and turned sideways. Luckily, the beach was made of small rocks and sand rather than boulders like the ones that riddled the bay, so other than being planted firmly on the beach and rocked back and forth by each wave, there was no damage to the boat. My dad's brother had a thirty-two-foot aluminum boat similar to mine anchored not far from where I drifted ashore, so I immediately radioed him for help, and he came to my rescue.

He got there as quick as he could, but as he was attempting to float a rope to me, he got the rope tangled in his propeller, and his boat immediately washed ashore just feet in front of me. Now both our boats were on the beach with a fifty-mile-an-hour wind holding us in place. There wasn't anything we could do but wait for the tide to go out.

By the time it did, the wind had died down some. My friend's family owned a fleet of power scows and landing crafts. I recognized one of their seventy-five-foot-long power scows. It was nearly thirty feet wide, with three engines. They were using it as a tender and had been anchored in the bay waiting for the period to end before anchoring in a more convenient location. Now they were waiting out the storm like everyone else.

I had worked on and around my friend's family's fleet of boats most of my life, so I was familiar with the boat I could see anchored in the bay. I walked out to the tender to see who was running the boat. One of the crewmembers was on watch when I got out to the tender, and he told me my friend was running the boat and was sleeping up in the captain's quarters next to the driving station. I woke him up and told him of my predicament, and he helped me devise a plan to stretch ropes out from both my boat and my uncle's boat and anchor the end of the line to a buoy. The plan was for him to come pick up the line and pull us off one at a time—providing the wind continued to drop off.

Thankfully, the wind cooperated, and as promised, when the tide came back in, my friend brought the power scow over to our location, picked up my uncle's line first, and pulled him off with relative ease. When he attempted to pick up my line, however, he managed to get it wrapped up in one of his propellers. I had to cut the line so he could go back out into the bay and go dry again to cut the rope out of his prop.

That left me sitting on the beach for another tide. I re-rigged the ropes and buoys, and helped cut the rope out of the propeller. On the next tide, he came and picked up the line and pulled us off without any further problems. All the herring was rotten by now, and we had no choice but to go out into deep water and shovel all 19,000 pounds overboard. We then went and found our net we had left behind. It was rolled up in a tight little ball sewn together with rotten herring. All we could do is strip the cork line and lead line off the web to salvage what was left of our remaining gear. By this time, the herring had all spawned, and herring season was over.

Electing not to try my hand at spawn-on-kelp, I limped back to Dillingham embarrassed by the whole ordeal I had gone through and vowing to never go herring fishing again. It was a long twelve-hour ride back to Dillingham, and I had plenty of time to reflect on the experience.

I once again thanked God for a safe outcome, and I even had a minute to step out on the deck in private to thank Joe for his protection, and for the calming feeling I got from knowing he was with me.

Chapter 16

JOE LETS ME LEARN THE HARD WAY

In the mid 1980s, my dad purchased a M-7 Maule Rocket with a 235-horsepower Lycoming engine. I was given the opportunity to fly it in support of the herring fishery. The Maule was a brand-new single-engine aircraft with a high-wing tail-wheel configuration, and it only weighed 1,500 pounds empty. It was around twenty-three feet long and had a wingspan of thirty-three feet.

I hadn't tried my hand at herring fishing since the spring with the unforgettable storm. I had been flying the Cherokee Six and the Cessna 206 for several winters now but hadn't had the opportunity to fly in support of the herring fishery because of my lack of experience. The herring fishery was spread out from Kulukak Bay to Hagemeister Island. Hagemeister Island is located at the southwest boundary of the Togiak herring district, which lay basically between these two landmarks and was geographically the extent of Yute Air's involvement in the herring fishery. From that area, the fishery moved farther west and out of range.

There were two processors anchored near Hagemeister Island, and I was assigned the responsibility of servicing both of these processors. On the west side of the island and toward the south end, there was a beach that was shaped like a banana. My dad warned me that it was steep compared to other beaches in Bristol Bay. Normally beaches in Bristol Bay aren't steep, and they are often in good shape.

The Maule was the only airplane my dad would let operate off this short stretch of beach, so I was solely responsible for servicing the two processers. The processers normally didn't travel with the processing employees on board; they were flown in to the processer after it arrived at the location. It was going to be my responsibility to fly all their people in and out and generally support the processers.

I didn't know exactly what I was facing out at the island, so I got a friend to go with me. We flew out to the island, where I spent a few hours getting comfortable with the beach. Before I knew it, I was flying from seven in the morning until ten at night trying to keep up with the demands of the two processers.

I soon discovered that to avoid getting hit by other airplanes, it was essential to fly low. The downside to that theory was the birds. Before long, I had a cockpit full of seagull feathers and the smell of pulverized bird. Thankfully, the bird hit the screen for the cabin air intake rather than some other area of the wing that would be time-consuming to repair, so after replacing the screen, I was back in business. I dodged a few more after that but never hit any more birds that summer.

I started getting a swollen head and feeling like I was just about as good as one could get in the Maule. I started getting in a big hurry and even concluded that I was wasting my time taxiing all the way out to the runway. I would just take off from my parking spot. I wonder where Joe was for that one. I was soon shut down by the airport manager and knocked down a peg or two.

The setback was only temporary, and soon my head was swollen once again. I started landing on beaches without looking them over for their overall condition—I guess to make up for all the lost time taxiing in Dillingham. This bit me in the backside when I attempted to land on a beach with big waves of piled sand and gravel mixed into a nice camouflaged trap for my ego. I really couldn't see the waves until the last second. I touched down, and the Maule porpoised once or twice and started to go over on its back.

In that situation, you don't have many options. You can pull the power off and flip over gently onto your back to minimize damage, or you can do something radical that will either work out in your favor or crash in such a way that there will undoubtedly be substantial damage. Not wanting to admit defeat, I pulled the yoke back as hard as I could and gave it full power. The tail came down like it had hit an invisible force field or something. The Maule bounced a few times violently and then came to a stop. Joe was on his game that day.

I got out, walked the beach, and discovered that if I had just taken the time to fly over, I would have seen that down closer to the water, the beach was much smother. I repositioned the Maule down near the water where the beach was smoother before I loaded the passengers. I was then able to get out of there without any more trouble.

The next day, I was sent to Hagemeister Island, with a stop at a fish and game spike camp at Kulukak Bay. When I arrived with a very urgent package for them, no one was there. So I decided to go out to Summit Island, where they had a more permanent camp.

Summit Island was small, just three miles long and a mile wide at its widest section. The island was situated northwest to southeast, with coves on both sides of the island in the middle. It was a great place to hide a boat if you got caught in a storm. In fact, in the storm I weathered the year I tried herring fishing, many boats had ended up at Summit Island.

The cove on the north side in the middle of the island had a beach. The beach was short and had several big rocks scattered throughout the landing area, but I felt I was up to the challenge. This time, after my near disaster inland, I decided to look over the beach. The biggest concern I had was that in the middle of the landing area, there was a rock that stuck up out of the sand a little over a foot. It was low tide, and at the end of the landing area, there was an insignificant creek that I figured was not a threat—rather an overrun area, if need be.

I flew over the beach one last time and made up my mind to land on the ocean side of the big rock, touch down before the rock, and upon reaching the rock, lift the wheel up, over, and back down on the other side—just like I had done years ago along the Izavieknik River in Little Yeller. I had looked over the area and had made a reasonable plan. Planning was everything, I had recently learned at the school of hard knocks.

I made my approach tight to the rocky cliff. When I felt I had enough speed to float to the beach, I cut the power. I touched down before the rock, cranked the aileron hard left, and kicked the right rudder to keep the airplane going straight. The wheel lifted and bounced off the top of the rock before settling back down on the beach. I was going faster than I had anticipated, but unlike Little Yeller, the Maule had good brakes. I was using them aggressively—something I don't normally do on a beach.

I was rapidly running out of room, and it looked as though I was going to plunge into the creek that no longer looked insignificant from where I was sitting. I pulled back on the yoke and dug deep into the brakes. As I got dangerously close to the creek, I let go of one brake, and just like I had done many times in Little Yeller, I ground-looped to a stop. Thank God the beach was as hard as a gravel road, or I would have flipped for sure.

I got out of the airplane, my legs weak from the experience. I had to take a few deep breaths as the realization that I had made a bad choice sank in, although at the same time I was excited about what I had just pulled off. Promising God that this particular thing would never happen again, I got the package and ran it up to the cabin. I left it in front of the door and ran back down to the beach to look at my tracks.

Now that I was safely on the ground, I started making plans to leave. I realized that there was no way to back-taxi for takeoff, so I had to take off back toward the rocky cliff I had squeaked by on landing. This time, my left wheel would have to be lifted up and over the rock. I said a quick prayer and then opened my eyes. I looked beside me toward the empty chair and said out loud, "Joe, I need you, buddy." My tail wheel was already in the creek because that's where it ended up on landing.

I took a deep breath, gave the throttle an aggressive push, and locked it in the full power position. I released the brakes and started to head for the rock. I started second-guessing whether I was going to have the momentum to get the left wheel up and over the rock, but just as I got there, I turned the aileron sharply to the right and kicked the left rudder to keep the airplane from diving into the ocean. The wheel lifted up, bouncing off the top of the rock and then back down onto the beach. Accelerating rapidly, I just needed an armload of flap, and I was safely on my way.

I headed on to my destination, Hagemeister Island, to do my pickup. It had taken longer to deliver the package than I'd figured it would, and now I was running late. As I headed out across Togiak Bay, I noticed that while I was working on my delivery, it had started to drizzle, with some light fog.

I could see what I thought was the north tip of Hagemeister Island. The Maule didn't have a working whiskey compass; in fact, the whiskey had steadily disappeared over the last several weeks. The compass was the only sort of navigation, but I was confident I was fine. This was the first time that I had even missed the compass. Normally, I was just following tree lines, mountain passes, or the coast.

It wasn't long before I realized the island I thought I was heading for was just a patch of heavy fog. Now I was starting to get scared. I was sitting there wondering how I had ended up in such a pickle so fast. I had grown up on the water, so I was confident I was going in a straight line and that I was heading for the island simply based on the fact that I was only feet from the water and the waves all looked to be rolling in a favorable direction. The fog got thicker and thicker, and I began to pray for guidance. The situation was getting serious.

I knew that Joe was with me, but even an angel would have a hard time getting me out of my predicament by himself, so I began to pray. It was a familiar prayer—one I had prayed many times over the years. I was scared to turn around because I would be heading for the unknown, possibly even a rocky cliff. With less than a quarter mile visibility, I feared I would hit something before I could turn and avoid it.

The waves I was flying just feet over were getting bigger and farther apart—a sign that I was in less-protected water. In other words, I was heading out to sea. I suddenly got an idea, or maybe Joe finally got through to me. I turned slowly to the right until I was heading with the waves. I had fished Togiak Bay enough to know that from where I estimated I was, the waves were most likely heading for the Togiak Village area. Once heading with the waves, I slowed down and pulled on a notch of flap. I felt better about heading in with the waves than I did about heading out toward Russia.

I flew literally feet over the water, navigating only by the direction of the waves. Before long, I noticed the waves getting closer together—a good sign that the water was not as deep. I figured I was coming up to the shore, but where? Moments later, I was over land, and I turned hard right to stay over the shoreline and follow it. I knew that by turning right, I was now heading north. Soon I began to recognize my surroundings, and before long I was coming up on the end of Togiak Airport.

Togiak Airport parallels the beach; in fact, the end of the airport I was heading for was practically on the beach. I was already slow, so when I saw the runway, I just pulled on the rest of the flaps and landed. Once I was safely shut down at the parking area, I noticed there were fifteen other planes on the runway that had all been chased to Togiak by the weather. They were all associated with the herring fishery in some way or another, and they were all exchanging stories about how they ended up in Togiak.

Out of embarrassment for the situation I had just survived, I kept my mouth shut. I walked up to the store and made a call to the company, letting them know what I was up to. I let them know I had delivered the package to Summit Island and that I was just waiting for the weather to lift so I could get out to Hagemeister Island to complete my mission. Soon the weather picked up enough that I felt I could get out to the island and resume my trip.

Before I left the ground, I apologized to God and Joe and thanked them for their help. That night, after returning home, I had a long talk with God and thanked him profusely for getting me out of that intense situation. I wanted to promise God that I would be more careful, but I knew that wasn't going to happen, and I was tired of breaking that particular promise. So I signed off with, "I'll try my best to stay out of trouble."

It wasn't long before I would be on my thirty-two-foot commercial fishing boat and would once again be calling on God and my overworked angel for continued support.

Chapter 17

ADRIFT WITH JOE

Now that I was a commercial pilot and owned my own thirty-two-foot fishing vessel, I was feeling all grown up. Like all young men, I was full of new ideas and better ways of doing things, and I had lots of energy to put my ideas to work. I was feeling adventurous, so I decided to try fishing the Egegik district.

The Egegik commercial fishing district was an eighty-mile boat ride to the southeast of Dillingham. It was one of five districts I could choose from with the commercial fishing permit I had, along with Nushagak, Naknek-Kvichak, Ugashik, and Togiak. Egegik was a small bay and better-suited to a slower boat like mine. Nushagak Bay was so large that I felt like a dog chasing its tail.

Over the years of fishing with my uncles, I was taught the gentleman's way of fishing. Fishing the boundary line in Nushagak Bay was all about taking turns. That's not how it was done in Egegik. I soon learned that fishing Egegik was more like combat fishery. Most of your fish were caught at the boundary lines, north and south. At the line, it wasn't uncommon to bump into another boat while jockeying into position for your shot at the fish as they entered the district, trying to swim up the river to spawn or sneak past to another river in another district.

My first experience with line-fighting in Egegik resulted in a small gash above my bunk. When you experience something like that, it makes you mad, but I learned from the experience and started to love the action. I was motivated by the wet bunk I slept on that month and vowed that this would never happen to me again. I learned a lot that year, but in the end, the whole experience turned me into a bit of a jerk.

I couldn't help but think about how relaxing it was to fish in Togiak Bay, so I decided that after the fast pace of the sockeye salmon season in Egegik, I would let my crew go home and drive the boat to Togiak to catch the coho salmon season. In Alaska, sockeye salmon are better known as reds and coho salmon as silvers. Togiak Bay was so laid-back that I would be able to fish alone and just relax.

Just as I had planned, I ended up in Togiak and had a successful and relaxing silver season. I decided to drive my boat back to Dillingham and put it up for the winter. I was out of supplies, and there was no easy way to restock my food or fill up with fresh water with a big boat like mine at the Togiak cannery. I headed to Dillingham without resupplying. I estimated the drive at about fourteen hours. My boat was equipped with a water tank, but it was empty and normally not for drinking. My drinking water was carried in a five-gallon gas jug, and it was less than half full. I had pilot crackers—a staple on any boat I had ever been on, providing you have peanut butter. I also had two cans of chili and a six-pack of pop. I figured this to be plenty of supplies for the trip back to Dillingham.

About seven hours into the trip, I smelled wires burning. When I opened my engine hatch, I could see why. I had an electrical fire in my engine room. The fire wasn't very big, so I was able to grab a pair of pliers that were sitting up on the dash by the steering wheel, jump down into the engine compartment, and disconnect the cables going to the battery. When I disconnected the cables, the engine quit.

There was a small fire extinguisher nearby, and I quickly extinguished the fire. Unfortunately, I didn't know a lot about wiring, and although I spent the next few hours trying to repair the damage, I was unable to restore the engine. I did manage to get a CB radio working, but not the VHF. The CB wasn't widely used, like the VHF, so I was unable to contact anyone. I tried to anchor, but the water was too deep; my anchor didn't touch bottom. I left it dangling in hopes that it would catch before I drifted ashore. It was raining, and from my location, I couldn't see the shore. I was confident that it wasn't that far away. It was dark by now, and I decided to get some sleep.

In the morning when I got up, I started to realize the seriousness of my situation. As usual when I found myself in a serious predicament, I went to my knees and prayed for help and guidance. It was comforting to know that Joe was by my side. Talking to Joe helped keep me calm, and because of that, I stayed focused on staying alive.

The visibility was extremely limited, and I knew that even though my dad was out looking for me, the idea that he would be able to spot me was wishful thinking. Over the next several days, I stayed busy doing everything I could think of to increase my odds of survival. I had a tide book and a wristwatch, so I knew when the tide was coming in or going out. I used a magnetic compass to determine that there was a slight offshore breeze. In the area that I believed I was in, I concluded that the tide would most likely parallel the beach more than it would travel toward the beach or away from the beach. Rather than let the wind blow me out to sea, I knew I needed to put out some type of a sea anchor.

The only sea anchor I had available to me was my fishing net. I fed out as much as I felt I could safely pull back in without the use of hydraulics. I was confident that by doing this, I would drift with the tide rather than letting the offshore breeze overpower the current and take me too far offshore to be seen by small aircraft flying the beach if the weather ever cleared up.

I had plenty of time to think while I was drifting through the fog. One of the things I would think about was something my dad said to me whenever I asked him when the weather would clear up enough for me to go flying. He would say, "I'm not sure when it will clear up, but one thing's for sure: it will indeed clear up. That much you can count on."

I took advantage of the rain whenever it fell. I would use a piece of plastic I tied strategically on the deck to funnel water into the five-gallon gas jug I used for my drinking water. I knew that staying hydrated would be a must, even after I ran out of food. I wasn't getting a lot of water, but it was enough to get me by.

I drifted for seven days before I finally got a good look at the shoreline. I was completely out of food by then; I was hoping something would swim into my net, but nothing ever did. I was only about a mile offshore, and after staring at the coastline for a while, I recognized my location as being about twenty-five miles from Dillingham.

The weather had cleared up considerably, but the wind was starting to blow harder offshore. I knew this was my best shot at being rescued. I was praying hard for someone to spot me. Even though I couldn't see him, I could feel Joe's presence and knew he was there with me and wouldn't let me down.

It wasn't long before I could see an airplane heading right for me. It was my dad's 1940s-model Grumman G-44A Widgeon. The Widgeon is a smaller, five-passenger version of the Grumman Goose, and over the years it had had several different types of engines, ranging from radial to horizontally apposed. My dad's Widgeon had Ranger engines. There are two types of hauls that a Widgeon can have: either a deep V haul G-44A or a flatter haul G-44. This Widgeon had the deep V and was slightly better suited to land in choppy water. It was thirty-one feet long and had a wingspan of forty feet.

Grumman Widgeon

The pilot who flew the Widgeon was one of the pilots I had idolized growing up. Without wasting any time, he landed in the choppy water. As the Widgeon slowed down and began to come off step, the waves were splashing completely up and over the fuselage of the airplane. The pilot didn't waste any time; he maneuvered the airplane right up to the back of the boat and shut off the engines. I didn't waste any time either. I jumped onto the nose of the Widgeon and pushed us away from the boat.

The Widgeon, just like the Goose, has a cavernous nose compartment that can be used for luggage. There was certainly enough room for me to ride comfortably inside. I opened the hatch leading to the baggage compartment and climbing down in as we drifted away from the boat. The pilot started the engines as I shut the hatch. Soon we were at full power, and I could feel us smashing into the waves. The engines were being splashed with so much water that you could hear them practically dying every time we smashed through a wave.

There was a little door between the nose compartment and the cockpit, and I opened it and stuck my head in as we splashed through the waves. I could see the controls going in all directions from stop to stop. I was hanging on to whatever I could as I felt us hit one last wave. The controls stopped moving near as much, and I could feel the Widgeon accelerating. I knew we were off and heading home.

Every seat in the Widgeon was full, and there was nowhere for me to go, so I just sat on the floor between the nose compartment and the front right passenger seat. That pilot set a new bar for me that day, and I prayed right then and there that someday, I would be as good as he was. When I arrived at Dillingham, my mom nursed me back to health with a homemade dinner and plenty of fluid. The next morning, my mom's brother took me out in his boat to retrieve mine—but when we arrived at the location where I had left it, it wasn't there. The wind had picked up that night and took it straight out to sea.

We called my dad on the radio and asked if he could use the Piper PA-31 Navajo and search for my boat. The Navajo is a cabin-class, twin-engine aircraft Yute Air used to move people, mail, and freight. It was a reliable aircraft to fly over water because of its ability to fly on just one engine. The Navajo was a seven-passenger airplane with an overall length of about thirty-two feet and a wingspan of forty feet. Dad searched for the boat at 230 miles per hour covering around five hundred miles without spotting the boat. The ocean is a big place, and the boat could have been hiding anywhere. I was just glad I wasn't still on board.

Two weeks later, we got a call from a friend at the Togiak cannery. He told us that he had gotten a radio call from a large vessel that was approximately forty miles offshore. They had found a boat practically sunk and had been successful in pumping it out. Not wanting to just leave it where they found it, they towed it to a protected area called Hagemeister Strait, northwest of Hagemeister Island.

There is a distinct point of land about four miles northwest of the northern tip of Hagemeister Island that is called Tongue Point. This was the general area we were told the boat had been anchored, with a 150-pound anchor using rope with no chain. Excited to hear the news, I jumped in Little Yeller and flew out to check on the boat. The closest village to where the boat was anchored was Togiak Village. My plan was to check on the boat and get its exact location, fly to Togiak, and get some boats to take me out and tow it back to the cannery where repairs could be made so I could attempt to get the boat back to Dillingham.

When I got to where the boat was supposed to be, however, it wasn't there. Instead, I found it beached on the coastline of Tongue Point. I landed beside the boat and inspected it for damage. It was in bad shape: the keel was bent, and there was other substantial damage that was going to require major repairs before it would move under its own power. There wasn't going to be anything I could do. Before flying back to Dillingham, I got down on my knees on the beach and thanked God for once again sparing my life and for assigning Joe to be my guardian angel.

I flew back to Dillingham and contacted my insurance company. They assured me that they could ship the boat to Seattle and get it fixed and back up to me in time for next season. The insurance company employed a small tugboat that was in

Dillingham. I used Little Yeller to support the rescue in any way I could, and soon the boat was on its way to Dillingham.

The boat was put on a barge and shipped to Seattle, Washington, where it was repaired and shipped back to me the following spring in time for salmon season.

Chapter 18

ANGELS WORK TOGETHER

Present Day Clarks Point

I had always had my eye on flying the Cessna 185, but my dad wanted me to get more time flying commercially in the Cessna 206, 207, and Cherokee Six before he would check me out in the Cessna 185. Unfortunately, before I had a chance to check out in the 185, one of my dad's employees found himself at Clark's Point in the airplane with a dead battery. Instead of asking for help from one of the villagers who was familiar with airplanes, he elected to prop-start the 185 by himself.

The way the story was explained to me, the pilot did not set his brakes or tie down the airplane—two major mistakes when prop-starting a 300-horsepower engine by yourself. My dad's Cessna 185 had a modified throttle mechanism. A standard throttle in a single-engine Cessna will be a round rod that comes out of the dash and would normally be longer than your middle finger—mine, at least. It is in the out position when the throttle is closed and is pushed in as the throttle is advanced. This 185 had no more than a two-inch throttle. The pilot cracked the throttle and then locked it in place. I'm not sure what if any effect that had on the aircraft on the ground, but in the air, the throttle will back down to idle if it's not locked into the desired position.

I found this out a few years later while checking a pilot out on a short dirt strip with thirty-foot trees on both sides and a lake at the end. The pilot I was checking out lifted off the runway, and while we were flying by, the trees were getting too close for comfort on my side. The pilot figured this would be a good time to let go of the throttle and drop the flaps abruptly. We might not have come so close to water-skiing the lake if the throttle had been locked into position instead of closing on its own at the same time the pilot dumped a big portion of our lift.

A small engine like the one on Little Yeller can be prop-started from standing on the right side of the airplane behind the propeller while holding on to something solid with your left hand; with your right hand, you can pull down on the propeller, turning the engine over. With a larger engine, it is best to stand in front of the engine and turn it over—the same direction, but from a more dangerous place to stand. When the pilot turned over the engine using the prop while standing in front of the aircraft, it started and was at nearly full throttle. The pilot threw himself to the ground as the airplane ran over him. The prop cut his coat in several places before the tail wheel nearly ran him over. The airplane, with nobody in it, made a tight arcing turn to the left, and just as it was leaving the ground, it flew into a nearby building.

Well, as you can imagine, it took a considerable amount of time to repair all the damage, but now the airplane was fixed and back online. I still hadn't heard anything about me being checked out in the aircraft, so I took it upon myself to get some experience on my own. The Cessna 185 did not have any controls on the right side, so I had never received any training in the airplane. One morning, I woke up and decided this was going to be the day I flew the Cessna 185.

It was late in the fall by now. Leaves had all fallen. It had snowed once or twice, but there was no snow on the ground. I rushed to the airport before anyone else showed up for work—especially my dad. I did preflight on the Cessna 185 and filled it up with fuel. I climbed in the left seat and made sure it was adjusted properly. I started it up and taxied away from the hangar to where I could do a run-up without being interrupted if someone did happen to come to work.

The engine checked out fine, so I took a deep breath and decided *this is it, this is going to happen.* I knew that if I used enough right rudder and kept the airplane going straight down the runway, the takeoff would not be a problem. I taxied out and departed on runway 19. The takeoff went smoothly, without any problems.

I knew enough about flying taildraggers to know that landing fast was going to be easier than landing slow. The first run I made down the runway was low and slow—only touching my wheel on the runway by accident. This helped me get a feel for where the runway was. The next run I made down the runway I touched a wheel, whether it be left or right, as many times as I could until running out of runway. The third run down the runway, I put my right wheel down on the runway and rolled it halfway down the field before switching over to the left wheel. I then went around for the last time.

This was it. I felt like I had built a perfect wheel landing. I could also see my dad's truck at the airport and knew I would be getting a call on the radio soon. Not wanting the extra pressure of my dad flicking his false teeth on the radio, I put the left wheel on the ground followed by the right and then looked far down the runway, slowly decreasing the power until it was all the way off. I used what I like to call my happy feet, and the airplane stayed right in the middle of the runway as the tail wheel gently came down.

Right on cue, I got a call from my dad. He said, "Okay, you proved your point. Come back in. I need the airplane." I did as I was instructed, and within a few weeks, I got a proper check-out in the airplane and started flying it to close villages so my dad could keep an eye on me.

In the winter, the Cessna 185 had wheel skis on it, and around February, we had a contract to haul reindeer meat off Hagemeister Island. The reindeer were under the management of some local reindeer herders from the village of Togiak, and every year the reindeer herders would harvest a carefully selected number of animals to sell to surrounding villages. We would pick up the meat from the island with the 185 on wheel skis and deliver the meat to Togiak Village. I finally got assigned this duty on the day after a heavy snow. I wasn't exactly sure where to land, and I knew full well what could happen if I hit another half-buried drum.

The reindeer herder who was on the island when I arrived was an older gentleman, and he had his snowmobile parked in a clearing when I flew over. As soon as he saw me fly over, he made several passes back and forth, marking a good area for me to land. I landed without any problems and loaded up the meat. I told him that the landing strip he had marked out wouldn't be long enough for takeoff with this load and the deep snow. He told me he would lead me. I figured he knew where the smoothest takeoff area was, so I agreed let him lead me and gave him a head start.

When he got far enough away that I didn't feel I would catch him, I started my takeoff. Everything was going great until he disappeared—but I was well underway by that point, and I just kept going in the direction where I had last seen him. I soon realized where he had gone: as I came up over a small rise, I saw that he had plunged into a snowbank and was stuck.

As I came over the rise, he was looking back over his shoulder at me with a horrified look on his face. I grabbed an armload of flaps and hopped over on top of him, settling back on the other side. I then continued my takeoff into the unknown. I plowed through a few more moguls, chewed up some alder brush with my prop throwing branches everywhere, and finally staggered into the air. I flew back over my fearless leader to make sure he was okay before heading on my way. He was just sitting on his sled smoking a cigarette. I took that as a good sign. There must've been some coordination between angels to pull that one off. As always, Joe was on his game.

Chapter 19

EVEN ANGELS GET HELP

My dad purchased a Britton-Norman BN-2 Islander from Great Falls, Montana. The Islander was a 1960s British high-wing cantilever monoplane with a rectangular fuselage and two wing-mounted piston engines perfect for passengers and cargo. It was thirty-five feet long and had a wingspan of forty-nine feet. With its incredible wing, it had a low stall speed of only forty miles per hour. It had a maximum range of 874 miles.

My dad asked me if I wanted to go down and fly it back up to Alaska with him. I never turned down an opportunity to go on a road trip, so of course I said yes. We picked up the airplane and headed up to Alaska.

I'll never forget the first landing in the Islander. The Islander sits level while on the ground, unlike anything we had ever flown. Most of the light aircraft we had flown sat slightly nose-high while on the ground. We experienced something different with our first landing in the Islander—the nose kept coming down further and further until we both instinctively lifted our feet up off the floor. It didn't take us long to get used to the feeling that we were landing without a nose gear, and we soon crossed the border into Alaska.

One thing about my dad's road trips—we were always on a shoestring budget. He even hated to spend money on gas, one of the essentials on a road trip. Our last leg between Northway and Anchorage was no exception. We had crossed the Canadian border into Alaska at Beaver Creek, Canada. From there we had flown to Northway, a popular stop for going through customs. We put on what my dad thought would be enough gas to get us the last four hundred miles into Anchorage—roughly half tanks.

From Northway, we went down the Nabesna River to Devils Mountain Lodge. We were flying low because the weather was rain and fog—not the best combination when flying through mountain passes and down rivers you don't see but once every few years. We flew past Gulkana, a small village on the Copper River, and pressed on, following the highway toward Palmer. We squeezed through a pass that, on the chart, was called Tahneta. If the airplane had a pause button, this is where I would have pushed it. Sadly, there wasn't any such thing.

Palmer was at the end of the mountain pass that my dad was navigating us through. He thought the weather through the pass that day was bad. For my part, I thought it was horrible. We were literally feet off the deck, not even seeing far enough ahead to turn around if need be. But feeling confident that my dad had everything under complete control, I wasn't worried.

When we finally got to an area of the pass that was wide enough and the weather was good enough that I felt we could turn around, I asked my dad a simple question; after all, he was the one holding the chart. I asked if he knew of any wires crossing the river between us and Palmer. The answer I got shattered any confidence I might have had about my dad being in complete control. His answer was, "I don't know."

I'm not sure what came over me, but after hearing his answer, I simply let go of the flight controls and put my hands up in the air. I must have been thinking that the investigators of our impending accident would relay to my mom that I wasn't flying at the time of impact. It wouldn't change the size of the spoon they'd used to scrape us off the dash, but it made me feel better for a few seconds.

My dad replied to this action with his disappointed voice and a deflated shoulder look. "Fine. Turn around then," he said. I didn't waste any time getting a good look at the bluff as I came around. Little did I know that by turning around, I had inadvertently made things worse. We were at a wide area of the Matanuska River, almost out of the pass—not the best place for me to have melted down.

Using a tone of voice that was confident and inspirational, my dad instructed me to keep circling in the wide area of the pass and climb up to 10,000 feet. I didn't see that one coming, but realizing that my last move wasn't the best and given the calm confident demeanor of my dad, I started to relax and did what I was told. My dad pointed out to me that we didn't have enough gas to get back anywhere; our only option was to get to Anchorage. He instructed me to stay on the instruments while he gave me directions that would keep us in the center of the pass as we climbed out.

I started to pray, and as I was asking for forgiveness for all my sins, I was also pointing out that this time it wasn't my fault. I was very familiar with my dad's climbing-out-of-the-mountain-pass story, and I knew just how wrong this plan could go.

Once we started to circle, patches of blue sky appeared. As we were climbing, my dad kept assuring me that he could see the ground and the mountains. It was beautiful up above the mountains. We called Anchorage approach, and they gave us radar vectors for an instrument approach. We broke out in plenty of time to land.

Flying a Visual Reference

The first thing I did when we got back to parking was to thank God for once again opening all the avenues that allowed us to safely arrive at our destination. The second thing I did was to look in the fuel cap holes to see if I could see any fuel. I don't think we could've started a fire by throwing a match through any of them—they were that dry.

I think this time, our angels got help from their boss because while the angels were lifting the aircraft safely up and over the mountains, God was clearing the weather for them.

The next day, I convinced my dad to put enough gas in the airplane to not only get us home but to also allow for a modest reserve. I'm sure I could convince him only because gas was cheaper in Anchorage than Dillingham, but no matter—I was happy.

Chapter 20

UNDER THE UMBRELLA OF AN ANGEL

It was springtime, and the herring fishery was in full swing. This year, my job was to fly a Cessna 206. Back then, all the Yute Air pilots got paid a percentage of what they brought in, so naturally all the pilots wanted to make as much money as they could. I wanted to fly the Cessna 207 during herring season, but my dad said because I was leaving to go salmon fishing after that, it wouldn't be fair to the pilots who were flying year around.

The Cessna 207 had a slightly longer fuselage than the 206 and could haul six passengers—one more than the 206. It also had a baggage compartment in front of the cockpit that helped balance out the airplane and keep the nose down to where the pilot could see out in front better at the beginning of the takeoff roll. My job was going to be flying back and forth between Nunavachak Beach and Dillingham.

Nunavachak Beach is about ten miles west of Kulukak Bay as a crow flies, but it's at least twice that by water because you must go out and around the right-hand point. Nunavachak Beach was in a large cove without any protection from storms, with strong southeast winds that come through in the spring. Large processors and tenders anchored in the cove in front of the beach where they could be serviced by small planes. The cove and adjacent beach looked like a small city. The entire area was bustling with activity.

Up above the main beach, there was a large flat area about a mile long and several hundred feet wide. The aircraft that flew overhead and directed the seine boats to the herring were called spotter planes, and they parked up on this flat spot. The pilots and their crew would set up tents up in this area. I loved what I was doing and was even starting to get a bit cocky. I was landing on the same area of the beach as the spotter planes and feeling like pretty hot stuff.

There was a new guy my dad had hired from the Lower 48 who had arrived in the fall of the previous year and had already proven himself to my dad. He was already checked out on the beach, and I was jealous of what the man had accomplished in such a short time. He had shown up in Alaska and been shown the mountain passes, but once checked out, he started doing things his own way. He would leave Dillingham and climb up high enough to clear the mountains, fly for a predetermined length of time, and let down on the other side. My dad loved it. I was intrigued by the methods he was using to get around but wasn't comfortable flying in the clouds in a single engine aircraft—especially after seeing him land with ice all over the airplane.

The old-timers had been flying through the mountains in horrible weather for so long it was second nature to them, and they weren't showing signs of joining him any time soon. The few pilots who were checked out in the twin-engine Navajo had been doing simpler-type flying for a while, but not in the single-engine aircraft. I wanted to be the type of bush pilot I had idolized all my life, so I convinced myself that his method of doing things would eventually come back to bite him in the leg, and I refused to listen to anything he had to say about it. Besides, my brain had been filled with what-ifs and "it's not *if* it's *when*" for so long that, frankly, I was too frightened to even entertain the thought.

Having proven that his way worked for him, the undeniable efficiency with which he accomplished his missions earned this pilot the nickname "Trip, trip." Because the 207 could haul one more person than the 206, I was making less money than him—and in some cases, with his bad-weather skills, he got the job done faster. The man knew that he was getting under my skin. He enjoyed getting me worked up, and like an idiot, I was letting him.

One morning, I was getting my airplane ready to head out to the beach to pick up a group of four when I ran into the new pilot at the gas pump. As I was climbing into my airplane, he said, "Don't crash." I would never say that to anyone—not even him. I tried to shrug it off, but it's just not something you want on your mind when you're heading out to do something inherently dangerous.

I left Dillingham and headed out to the beach to pick up my passengers. When I arrived at the beach, the group of four was waiting for me. As I was loading them into the airplane, a man approached me. He said he was a diesel mechanic and was looking for a ride to Dillingham. I had one empty seat and was thinking, *Great! More money,* so I said yes. The man then asked if I would hang on a minute while he grabbed his gear. Knowing it was going to inconvenience the group I had come after, but focused on keeping up with the money being made by the new guy, I said yes.

I walked with the mechanic down the beach to where he had his gear stashed. When I first looked at the gear, my first impression was, *Oh no, I'm not going to be able to take it all.* I instantly felt stupid for not catching the statements "diesel mechanic" and "my gear." I should've said no at that point, but greed and jealousy of the new guy was clouding my judgment. I just grabbed two of the heavy toolboxes and started hiking back toward the plane.

As I was walking back to the airplane, I was stumbling over small twigs and rocks, making me aware of how heavy the toolboxes were. I was a strong young man and wouldn't normally be tripping over things so easily. I suspected that all the tripping was Joe's way of telling me to apologize to the mechanic for not being able to take him and all his luggage to Dillingham and get underway without him. I had ignored Joe's advice in the past and regretted it later. This time he was really being persistent, and I was having a hard time ignoring him.

I loaded the toolboxes and the rest of the man's gear in the back of the airplane. I told him to hop in and put his seatbelt on. I shut the door, went around to the pilot-side door, and jumped into the pilot seat not feeling any better about my decision. The tide was going out, but it was still high enough that I only had a fifteen-foot-wide beach to work with. It had been plenty wide for landing because the nose was low and I could see, but now the nose was up high in the air because of the three tool boxes and the five passengers' luggage in the back of the airplane. I wouldn't be able to see in front of the airplane until I got going forty miles per hour—fast enough for the nose to come down.

There was a lot of activity on the beach, and keeping an eye on your surroundings was important. To make things worse, I had been flying with my seat lowered and leaned back. It was comfortable in the air, but it was hard to see over the dash with the nose high in the air and me being only five foot eleven. When I sit down on the seat, it was noticeably more uncomfortable than it had ever been in this position. By now, I was used to picking up on signs from Joe, and I could tell that Joe was trying to get me to rethink everything I was about to do. Once again, I ignored the signals.

I was trying very hard not too appear concerned about my predicament. There had been a large storm in the area recently that had pushed a large fuel tank way up on the beach. I'm sure it blew off the deck of one of the processors. It was up near the top of the beach and out of my way. I had enough room to get by, but it was a little intimidating because I wouldn't be able to see it until I was well underway.

After starting the engine, I attempted to get one last look at the beach. I nonchalantly stretched my torso and strained to look over the nose of the airplane. I settled back into my seat and applied full power. Just as I reached the speed where my nose started coming down, a skiff hit the beach in front of me. It was still about a quarter of a mile away, barely visible over the dash. I saw a man jump out of the boat. The man was running toward the top of the beach, dragging an anchor that was attached to a long rope.

My gut reaction was to jerk the throttle back, stop, and dump the mechanic and all his gear. Looking back, I can see now that the skiff coming to the beach at that exact moment was Joe's way of giving me one last chance to do the right thing.

My ego wouldn't let me shut down, however. Besides, I was encouraged by the fact that I was starting to see the beach in front of me. I could see that the man who had run the anchor up the beach had stopped and was now running the anchor back down to the boat. When he reached the boat, he immediately pushed it back off the beach as he jumped back in.

As I was watching the boat drift back away from the beach, I inadvertently drifted down the beach toward the water, and now water was spraying up from the right wheel onto the window. I pulled back the control wheel and kicked the rudder to the left, hoping that I could get back up onto the beach, but the water sucked me in. As the propeller struck the water, it instantly killed the engine.

Without the engine to drown out any of the horrifying sounds of the crash, I could hear the left wing dragging on the gravel as the airplane dove under the water. All I could see out any of the windows was water. After a few long seconds, we appeared to be floating. Gas was running down onto my left shoulder because the wing had been bent back significantly. This was also keeping my door from opening, and the only other exit available was the right rear door. I told the mechanic I had seated in front of the door to open it. He just sat there looking at me in disbelief.

With gas pouring down on my left shoulder, I said the next thing that came to mind, most likely from a movie I had watched recently: "It's going to blow." That got his attention, but when he tried to open the rear door, the flap was preventing the door from opening. We were trapped as water slowly filled the cabin. The flaps operated by an electric motor, and by the grace of God, the battery was still on and functioning. I reached down and pulled up on the flap actuator. The flaps came up, and the door flew open.

Everyone started piling out of the rear door. I was still sitting in my seat watching to make sure everyone got out okay. After everyone was out, I hurried to the rear door. Three of the people were already out of sight but two were still swimming. Knowing that the water would be extremely cold this time of year, I hesitated for a minute before jumping out. I wasn't looking forward to the swim to shore. I wasn't a strong swimmer, and with frigid water, I wasn't sure I would make it.

Just then, one of the swimmers stood up, and I realized that the water was only waist deep. I jumped into the water, instantly stunning my sensitive area, but the water didn't go up over my belly. Humbled and embarrassed, I grabbed a couple of toolboxes out of the back and started making my way toward shore. The mechanic met me halfway. I handed him the toolboxes and went back for another load. Everyone pitched in, and we unloaded the airplane with minimal damage to anyone's gear.

As I set down my last load, I was startled by the presence of a large man, probably six feet six inches tall, standing directly in front of me. I looked up at him, and I don't know why, but just looking at him made all my anxiety and humiliation temporarily go away. People were running to our location from every direction. Boats were coming to shore from virtually every processor anchored in the bay. The large man put his arm around me and said in a gentle and comforting voice, "Come with me. I will get you into some dry clothes."

The large man introduced himself as Joe. His gentle spirit and calming demeanor were exactly what I needed at that time. I let him lead the way to his tent up on the flat area amongst all the other tents. He pulled some clothes out of a duffel bag.

I was a size medium, and the man was triple X. He weighed at least three hundred pounds and looked like a body-builder. I didn't question him; I just took off my wet clothes and put the dry clothes on.

He handed me a rope. I tied it around my waist to hold up my new clown pants. He walked out of the tent and I, still in shock, followed the gentle giant back to the accident. By this time, there were at least two hundred people all down on the beach by the airplane.

The man never hesitated at all. He walked straight into the middle of the crowd. Not knowing anything else to do, I stayed tight to the man's side like a baby duck. In the middle of the crowd, it was so noisy. People were shouting. You could still hear motorboats coming to shore. I had never experienced anything like it.

For some reason, standing beside the large man was calming. Without him, I would have been trying to get away. As soon as he spoke to the crowd, I could tell that he was in complete control. He wasn't shouting, but his voice was loud and firm. The crowd went silent. He looked right at one of the men in the crowd like he knew him. He instructed the man to get his hundred feet of rope out of his boat. The man immediately turned, ran toward his boat, and promptly returned with a hundred feet of rope.

There was another man in the crowd with hip boots on. The large man looked at him and, with the same gentle yet commanding voice, instructed him to take one end of the rope and tie it to the ring on the bottom of the airplane tail. The man did as he was told.

Next, the large man instructed everyone to line up from the airplane all the way up and over the top of the beach. He told them to take the rope with them. With gentle yet firm words, this large man organized the largest game of tug-of-war I had ever witnessed. Then he gave the word to pull the airplane up to the top of the beach. The airplane, still full of water, came up the beach like they were pulling on an empty rope. Standing beside the large man was like being under an umbrella that was protecting me from everything that was going on.

Once the plane was up high enough on the beach that it wouldn't be in the way of any aircraft taking off or landing, the man ordered the crowd to disperse, and they did. The rope was disconnected, coiled up, and taken back to the boat. As quickly as the crowd had gathered, they were gone. I hadn't left the large man's side in over an hour, yet now as I looked around, even he was gone. I hadn't even thanked him. I found myself standing on the beach in the exact spot where I had first set eyes on the large man.

I felt as if the whole thing had been a bad dream. As I stood there trying to make sense out of the last couple of hours, a man approached me who I recognized as being one of the managers from a processor. He asked me if I would like to go out to the processor and use the radio to make the dreaded call. I accepted and soon found myself in front of a high-frequency radio. I didn't know exactly what to say. I had made plenty of calls back home with bad news, but this was the worst news I'd ever had to deliver.

I'm sure that there had been plenty of chatter on the HF radio about a crash because all I had to tell my dad was that I got the radios wet in his airplane, and within an hour he showed up in a 207 piloted by the man who had told me not to crash. My dad walked right up to me with a can of paint stripper and a paint brush in his hand. He handed them to me, and the first words he spoke to me were, "Get my name off that aircraft." He had brought a mechanic with him who went right to work removing anything of value.

I never saw the large man again, but will never forget him for as long as I live. He had introduced himself to me as Joe, and coincidence or not, as far as I'm concerned, that large man was my guardian angel. That night, safely back home, I had a lot to pray about.

I had let greed and jealousy get in the way of good judgment, and I asked God for forgiveness. Accepting full responsibility for putting not only my life in danger but the lives of my passengers, I was deeply grateful that God had once again spared my life and given me another chance to prove myself as a pilot.

Not wanting to forget the skills I had learned from the bush pilots, I was willing to accept the fact that there might be other ways of doing the same job. Times were changing, and it was up to me to accept the change or go on living in denial.

I wasn't ready to start flying single-engine airplanes in the clouds, but I was willing to entertain the idea that at least for some people, this was a way to safely get around Alaska effectively. I had no reason to be jealous. I had mastered what I had set out to learn. It was time for me to be open-minded about other ways of doing things. In the past, I had gathered information from a variety of sources to draw my own conclusion. This was no different.

I was changing the way I used the radio, and now I would keep an open mind about new ways of getting around Alaska. I would simply make a rational decision as to whether it was something I wanted to adopt or not.

Chapter 21

JOE AND I FACE A BEAR

It was summer again, and time to go commercial fishing. I decided to head back to Egegik for another year of line-fighting. After sleeping on a wet bunk the first year I fished Egegik, I had made some radical modifications to the boat. The modification that was the most noticeable to the other fishermen was the three-quarter-inch plywood I put over all the windows while fighting the line. I did this so that the windows wouldn't be broken by someone's boat scraping by or some other mishap.

The modification that was the most intimidating was the four-inch tube that I had welded through the bow of the boat and pulled a fifty-pound anchor shank up through, leaving the fluke palms of the anchor protruding out past the bow. I never intended to ram anyone on purpose, but it was a very effective intimidation tool and a great way to keep my bunk dry when I bumped something by accident. I had also removed my nice-looking flying bridge driving station from up on top the cabin and replaced it with a fully enclosed driving station that looked more like an outhouse. I constructed it out of quarter-inch aluminum so it would at least slow a bullet down if I happened to run across anyone with road rage.

With the outhouse on top of the boat, I could spend all day out of the weather with a great view of everything that was going on. I had also learned that to have complete control over your net, it was imperative to tie your lead rope to the top of your antenna mast. This allowed the boat to turn 180 degrees in either direction in order to avoid obstacles if necessary.

As I was leaving Dillingham, the fog started to roll in, but it wasn't very thick. I could see well enough to avoid other boats. My boat was equipped with a Loran-C navigation system, but it didn't have a radar. A radar displays other boats on a monitor and helps the driver to avoid a collision. The Loran-C triangulated your position using three ground stations and was the best source of navigation for Bristol Bay at the time.

The tide was just starting to go out when I left the Dillingham boat harbor, so I would have the extra push of the tide for the first four hours of the trip. My plan was to head south down past Nushagak Point. I planned to follow the channel out past Etolin Point, where I could head directly toward Egegik Bay. I had been living in my boat at the harbor getting it ready to head out fishing, so the sink was full of dirty dishes. The boat was equipped with an autopilot that didn't get used all that often, but I had planned to use it on this trip because I was traveling alone. I had hired out-of-state crew for the upcoming season, and they were going to fly to Egegik Village by small airplane after arriving in Alaska. I planned to pick them up from the dock at Egegik.

As I approach Clark's Point, a popular anchorage for large and small vessels during the summer, the fog started to thicken. I didn't notice because I had elected to get the dishes done while traveling. I had turned on the autopilot and was standing at a sink that was only feet from the steering wheel. When my boat cut through a wave created by a nearby boat, I looked up just in time to see the view out of the front window starting to turn green.

I took one step toward the steering wheel and grabbed it with my left hand. With my right hand, I turned off the autopilot. It was clear to me at that moment that I was going to run straight into a small wooden power scow on my port bow. The sixty-five-foot-long two-engine wooden power scow was about twenty-five feet across the bow and was on anchor right in front of Clark's Point Village. The scow's bow was the same height as mine and was flat across the front like a barge. I had just enough time to turn the boat enough to impact the scow on its port corner with my port corner. Pieces of green wood went flying everywhere as my chest slammed up against the dash hard enough to knock the wind out of me.

The small scow was hit so hard the impact moved it out of my way, and now I was sliding down its port side. The scow had large dump-truck tires chained up along each side that were used as bumpers. I was hitting every one of them and throwing them up onto the scow's deck as I slid by. Behind the scow, there was a thirty-two-foot wooden fishing boat that was hanging back about fifteen feet by a rope. When the scow moved over, the wooden boat stayed where it was, and now I was in danger of hitting that head-on.

There was a man on the boat who had apparently come outside to have a morning smoke when I hit the scow. When I first saw him, he was hanging onto the cabin of his boat with his free hand and hanging onto his cigarette with the other. His face had a very confused yet terrified look. Just before I slammed head-on into the man's boat, the rope came tight, and his boat turned just enough that I collided with the port side of his boat with the port side of mine. Seconds later, I was in thick fog again.

I got the boat turned around to where it wasn't traveling with the current anymore and started surveying the boat for damage. Besides a large dent in the aluminum bumper up by the reinforced bow, there was no structural damage. Having learned the lesson that Joe taught me about morals while flying in crop-duster country, I sheepishly and cautiously drove back to the scow to apologize and make sure everyone was okay. The crew on the boat was very understanding, and after I promised to bring them a bottle of booze, we exchanged details of the event, like the crew being tossed out of their bunks onto the ground and truck tires being tossed twenty feet to the other side of the scow. I cautiously got back underway.

I was recognized by the other fishermen who fought the line at Egegik and had earned the reputation of being a real jerk. Once I arrived at the fishing grounds, it didn't take me long to get back into character. In my mind, being good at fighting the line was not the same as being a good fisherman—at least not in the way I was taught by my dad and uncles. To be effective at fighting the line, you had to be unpredictable, and it didn't hurt for people to believe you weren't thinking clearly.

One of my favorite tricks to use while trying to be the first one in position to set my net out on the line was to pretend I didn't have any reverse and that I wasn't going to be able to stop. This usually only worked once during each feeding frenzy, so I would use it strategically. Because of the extremely intimidating bow and the five tons of aluminum that would appear to be out of control at about four knots, it was in the best interest of anyone who was in my way to move. I had two crew members; one was a friend of mine from Washington State and the other was a bodybuilder from Oregon. We were all good at working together.

One of the things that was unavoidable while fighting the line was getting nets tangled together. The real trick was untangling your nets without losing any fish. One day I found myself stern-to-stern with a fiberglass boat. The captain of the fiberglass boat had accidently backed over his own net while trying to tow his net from one of his stern cleats. Without control of his boat or his net, he had managed to tangle his net with ours, and fish were still hitting the tangled nets, sowing them together.

The captain of the other boat wanted us to use our engine to tow our nets apart so he could get his net back in his boat before he drifted outside the fishing boundary and got a ticket. I had a better idea. I was pulling both of our nets into my boat and picking all the fish out, keeping them for myself. I was going to give him his net back when I was finished. It was a little choppy that day, so every time my aluminum boat would contact the fiberglass boat, he lost chunks of his boat into the water. They were small chunks, but the boat owner was screaming and shouting at the top of his lungs from the back of his boat for us to use our engine to pull the two nets apart.

We were satisfied with just ignoring him because the way we saw it, he was the one who put himself in this predicament in the first place. That is, until he grabbed a knife and acted like he was going to jump into the back of our boat. This wasn't going to work for us, so without hesitation, I gave the order to stand by to repel boarders—something that I always wanted to say on a boat.

That got his attention, but by now, he was standing up on the back of his boat holding onto his roller with one hand and the knife in the other. Simply put, the roller was normally a four-foot-wide hydraulic drum that was about a foot or more in diameter. On each side of the roller were posts that ran perpendicular to the drum with rollers of their own that helped guide the net in or out of the boat. It didn't look like he was serious about jumping on board; it looked more like he was trying to intimidate us. So I tried an intimidation tactic of my own.

It was a warm sunny day, and we were all working in just our slicker bottoms and T-shirts. I ordered my bodybuilder to rip off his T-shirt. This guy loved showing off his body and didn't hesitate to grab his T-shirt with both hands and rip it off. The shirt ripped in half, and he let the cloth fall to the deck. The owner of the fiberglass boat jumped back inside his boat and put down his knife. He had a few choice words for us, but when his yelling started to resemble yelping, the Christian side of me came out. I put the boat in forward and pulled our nets apart. Unfortunately, when I did that, his net flew out over our roller in one big matted clump for him to work on at his leisure.

We fought a furious battle that year and at the end of the season, I was missing the relaxed atmosphere of Togiak Bay. During one of the closures, I met and managed to befriend some fishermen from Pilot Point, located near the mouth of the Ugashik River about forty-five miles south of Egegik. The Ugashik River flows into Ugashik Bay. The Ugashik Bay district tends to have a slightly later run of red salmon, but when they show up, they come in large numbers all at once.

My new friends told me that the Ugashik district would be a great place for me to fish silvers, a slightly larger fish than the red that shows up in smaller numbers after the red run. I described to them what fishing was like in Togiak, and they told me about a favorite spot of theirs farther south of Ugashik called Cinder River. Cinder River is about twenty-five miles farther south of Ugashik Bay and is quite small and tricky to navigate with a thirty-two-foot boat, especially if you don't know the area. They described it as a laid-back and relaxing place to fish, and they thought I would enjoy fishing there.

They said I could hang with them, and they would show me the ropes. The whole idea appealed to me, so when the season ended in Egegik, I let my bodybuilder go back home to Oregon. My friend from Washington State and I followed our new friends down to Ugashik Bay. When we arrived, the silvers hadn't shown up yet, so we all held up in a protected area called Dago Creek.

Dago Creek is a small river that flows into Ugashik Bay four miles west of Pilot Point, with a road connecting the two. It was too early to go down to Cinder River, so my new friends invited us to tag along on an illegal venture to catch reds that were still milling around the lower Ugashik River. They made the whole thing sounds daring and exciting.

It didn't take too much convincing for me to agree, and we soon found ourselves up in the river just before dark. We followed our new friends' lead and anchored one of our three fifty- fathom nets along the river. We had an eight-foot inflatable runabout with a fifteen-horsepower motor on it that we carried onboard with us all summer. The boat was used primarily to run back and forth to shore, but in this case, we were going to use the boat to keep the fish picked out of our net that was anchored along the river. It didn't take both of us to run the boat to shore and pick the fish out of the net, so we took turns.

It was a clear night, and the moon was lighting up the area just enough for us to take the boat ashore and remove the few fish we were catching from our net. I didn't have a gun with me on the boat, but my fishing partner did. He owned a stainless-steel .44 Magnum pistol with an eight-inch barrel. He had already taken a turn at picking the fish out of the net; when it was my turn, he told me to take his gun with me.

At first, I refused, not wanting to get his gun wet or possibly even drop it in the water, but he insisted that I take it. Getting a strong feeling that Joe wanted me to accept my partner's offer, I put the gun in the boat and headed for shore. When I got to where I thought the net would be, it wasn't there. I knew I had to be in the right area, so rather than use the boat to run up and down the river, I elected to walk.

It wasn't your typical beach. The bank of the river was about two feet higher than the water. Clumps of dirt and grass that had been ripped off the shoreline by the spring ice had been deposited randomly up on the edge of the bank. There were cracks and deep holes that made walking up out of the water hazardous, especially at night, so I elected to walk along the shore in the water. The soil under the water was firm, and walking was easy.

As I was splashing along the shoreline, I started getting this eerie feeling that I was being watched. I stopped and scanned the shoreline for any movement. I tightened my grip on the gun, not wanting to drop it into the water at this point. I knew there were a lot of bears in the area, but I hadn't given it much thought until now. The bears around the Ugashik district are Alaska Peninsula brown bears and range in weight between 800 and 1,200 pounds. I couldn't see any reason to be alarmed, so I continued.

I was keeping a close eye on the clumps of grass that were up on the edge, and at one point, I could swear one of the clumps of grass moved. I stopped dead in my tracks and stared at it. I must've stood there frozen for at least two minutes, but nothing moved. I dismissed the whole thing as my imagination and started to splash again. As soon as I started to move, the clump of grass started to move—but this time, the clump of grass was closing the distance between us at an alarming rate. I froze in my tracks and turned to face what was obviously a charging bear.

I held the .44 Magnum with both hands and pointed it straight at the charging animal. I had never shot a .44 Magnum or a bear before. I knew that if I didn't hit the bear just right, I wasn't going to get it stopped before it reached me. I was only twenty feet from the shoreline when the bear leapt off the edge and landed in the water.

When he landed in the water, it was like the loudest belly-flop you can imagine. Water was still in the air from the gigantic splash as I squeezed the trigger on the .44 Magnum. As I was pulling, the trigger the gun lowered and went off with an echoing sound that pierced the darkness like the thunder associated with a flash of lightning. It illuminated an eight-foot bear that, from my angle, looked like a two-story building. The bullet struck the water between the charging bear and where I stood frozen in my tracks.

I just stood there paralyzed with fear as I saw the bear make a sharp right just feet in front of me. The bear had gotten so close to me I could smell him. I watched the bear jump up onto the bank and disappear into the dark night. I must've been holding my breath the whole time because I suddenly gasped for air.

I splashed back to the inflatable without taking my eyes off the clumps of grass on the bank. I quietly thanked God for saving my life. When I got back to the boat, I thanked my partner for the use of his gun and promised to buy one of my own when we got back to civilization. I explained to him how I felt about fishing up in the river, and he agreed that it was time we call it a year and head home.

We didn't end up at Cinder River that year, but I didn't take it off the list of possibilities for the future. I asked God to forgive me for fishing illegally and apologized to Joe and thanked him for being there for me when I needed him most.

My partner and I went back to the beach and pulled up our fifty-fathom net and anchors. I never went back up the river to fish illegally. I know that Joe lowered the gun for me that night. I hate to think about what might have happened if I had wounded the bear.

We make our own choices in life. All our angels can do is send us feelings and other signs—some subtle and some unmistakable. After doing everything they can to stop us from making mistakes, they stand beside us and do what they can to protect us, even if it means lowering a gun to do it. Once again, I had gone down a bad road but had been given yet another opportunity to make better choices in life, and once again I vowed to do just that.

Chapter 22

ANGLES FLEW MY AIRPLANE

A few months after returning from another great fishing season, despite having been mistaken for a caribou, I bought my very first brand-new snowmobile. After breaking it in, I was anxious to see how fast it would go. I was thinking that the airport would be the best place to open it up and see what it would do.

Early in the morning was the best time to ride your snowmobile at the airport without getting caught by the airport manager, so on my way to work, I took one of the back trails that led to the airport. It had snowed the night before, and the plow trucks were already on the airport and taxiway. My timing was perfect. The plow truck that was at the airport was way down at the north end, and the plow truck that was plowing the taxiway wasn't in sight. I got onto the airport at the south end and proceeded northbound as fast as the machine would go. The speedometer wound up to nearly eighty miles an hour before I shut it down.

I turned around before the plow truck on the north end could spot me and opened it up heading back toward the south. As I approached the taxiway, I slowed down and drifted around the corner, heading for the hangar. My body was postured in an aerodynamic racing stance as I smashed the throttle against the handlebars. As I let go of the throttle and started to slow down, I glanced down at my speedometer. It was reading just over sixty miles per hour. I looked back up just in time to see myself hit the edge of where the plow truck had stopped plowing. The plow truck only plowed state property; the property in front of Yute Air was my dad's responsibility.

As the front of the snowmobile came to a stop, the backside of the snowmobile turned into a catapult that sent me flying upside down and backward. As my helmet hit the ground, my legs still straight up in the air, I had a front-row seat as my brand-new snowmobile hit the ground. I wasn't concerned about my own safety or even the fact that I was sliding through a foot of snow on my helmet upside down and backward. My only concern was how many pieces of my new snowmobile were going to fly off in front of my eyes before it was all over.

I managed to stay out in front of the snowmobile and started tumbling along like a rag doll. I came to a stop without any broken bones and ran to what was left of my snowmobile. It was upside down and still running.

I turned the snowmobile over and started to survey the damage. It was considerable, but despite both skis being bent up at a ninety-degree angle from hitting the abrupt edge and the cowling about ten feet away in two pieces, I could limp it over to the hangar and hide it in one of the corners. As the adrenaline wore off, I realize that I had sprained my right foot. It was painful to put pressure on.

We had gotten a lot of mail the night before for the village of New Stuyahok. This was a small village about sixty miles up the Nushagak River, but it was only a little over forty miles in a straight line. I had helped unload the mail off the DC-6 the night before and had already received permission to start moving the mail in the Islander. The Islander was hauling about two thousand pounds a trip.

Despite my physical injuries, I knew it was important for the company to get the mail moved before the weather changed for the worse. I had a good friend who I had soloed on his sixteenth birthday in one of Yute Air's Cherokee Sixes. He had worked for my dad in trade for the use of the airplane. He was my first student after receiving my instructor rating. By this time, he had received all the ratings necessary to fly for a family friend who had a small air taxi on the south end of the ramp. I knew if he wasn't busy, I could count on him to help me out.

I drove the forklift to where he was working, and sure enough, he was there hanging around waiting for something to do. I asked him if he would like to get some Islander time and help me haul some mail. He eagerly said yes, and I gave him a ride back to Yute on the forklift. When we got back to the hangar, I used the forklift to deliver a 3,800-pound pallet of pop out to the airplane.

As we loaded the Islander, we started talking about what I had overheard the chief pilot and another FBO operator saying about the Islander: that the more weight you put in the back of the Islander, the better it flies. I was easily influenced by whatever the old-timers had to say, and I might have taken their statements a little too literally.

We started to load the plane, and the next thing I knew, we had put nearly a thousand pounds of pop in the four-hundred-pound-max baggage compartment in the rear of the Islander. I'm not sure exactly how much pop we stuffed into the Islander that day, but out of the 3,800 pounds I brought out to the plane, only a short stack was returned to the mailroom. We had weight and balance forms already filled out for maximum loads to various locations that we frequented, so I signed my name to one for our destination, and we were on our way.

The Islander only had brakes on the left side, so we decided that it would be best for my friend to fly from the left seat because of my severely sprained right foot. Given the fact that we were overweight, yet ignoring the fact that we were severely aft of our center of gravity (CG), we decided to use runway 19 for departure. We elected not to use any flaps for departure, thinking speed would be more beneficial than lift given our current situation.

Nothing seemed out of the ordinary as we left the ground and headed up the river. I was starting to feel the effects of my tumble and was content to just sit there and relax. I was confident that I had made the right decision not to miss work and was grateful for my friend's help. We discussed how we were going to land at New Stuyahok and decided that it was in our best interest to make our approach straight in rather than to overfly the field and enter a normal traffic pattern. After all, now that most everyone was at least listening to the radio if not transmitting their intentions, the radio would be a big advantage for us today. A company 207 answered our call and told us to go ahead and land first.

Back then, the New Stuyahok runway was up on a hill, with the south end of the runway on the edge of a two-hundred-foot cliff. A large ravine ran nearly perpendicular to the end of the runway, and the creek at the bottom of the ravine dumped out into the Nushagak River. We were on a long final landing to the north, still at cruise power and about eight hundred feet above the airport elevation. We started to slow down, and everything looked great. I could see the company 207 holding out to the east.

I gave the order to put the first position of flaps down. The Islander had two flap positions: half and full. The aircraft stabilized as forward trim was applied, and I was pleased with the way my friend was handling the plane. I was even giving myself a pat on the back for doing such a good job teaching him to fly. I was also convinced that we had found the secret to loading the Islander.

At about two hundred feet above the airport elevation, I gave the order to put down full flaps. I was just sitting there with my arms folded, pleased with the way things were turning out, when my friend turned to me and said in a calm voice, "Les, I think something's wrong."

"Wrong? What's wrong?" I asked, startled.

"We are out of forward trim, and I can't push the controls forward," he answered.

On any other airplane I had ever flown, when you ran out of trim, you still had more elevator travel. I grabbed the controls to help push them forward, but they wouldn't budge. I grabbed the trim to try to roll it forward, but it wouldn't budge either. I reduced the flaps to half because the flaps were the last thing that we had touched. We started sinking down toward the bluff that the airport was built on.

I felt that we were going to hit the bluff if I didn't do something, and I didn't think that pulling back the power was going get the nose down in time to help us get back under control, so I shoved the prop control levers and throttles up against the firewall. The nose slowly started to rise even higher, so I pulled up the remainder of the flaps. The nose finally stopped coming up—but it wasn't coming down either. We were still gaining altitude, so I felt we had at least bought ourselves some time to think.

By now, we were both pushing on the controls and trying to trim forward, but it wasn't helping. I had all the engine controls pushed hard against the firewall. Time began to slow, and the noise of our engines and props thrashing at the air started to fade like the volume was being turned down. It felt like we were climbing up a cliff filled with loose rocks. We had managed to claw our way up to about six hundred feet above the airport, but we were getting dangerously close to stalling.

I remember my friend and I looking at each other, and it felt like we were having a complete conversation. As the airspeed dropped even lower, we said, simultaneously, "Goodbye." We were at about seven hundred feet above the airport elevation at this point, and it was time to make our next move. Feeling like we were out of options, and with my fingers still wrapped firmly around the throttle, I thought about pulling it back in hopes that the nose would drop and give us an opportunity to get the plane flying again before we hit the ground.

I was waiting for what I felt was the very last second before making my move. Suddenly, though, the airplane made an abrupt move of its own. With all the flight controls still locked full forward, the airplane turned sharply to the left and the right wing flew up and over, like I had seen crop dusters do in Arizona. It felt as if there was an angel on each wing tossing us about like we were a toy. We ended up with our nose pointing nearly straight down, diving toward the ravine that led to the river. As we got closer to the ground, the control wheel started coming back, and we both got this overwhelming feeling that everything was going to be okay.

The company 207 that was waiting for us to land started to question our intentions. We ignored him and gently started to bring the plane out of the dive. We used every inch of the altitude that we had, pulling out more than a hundred feet below the airport elevation and only inches before hitting the ground. We had been holding our breath the whole time, and now we were sucking down oxygen like we were stocking up on it.

As we flew down the ravine in ground effect, we answered the pilot in the 207 by simply telling him that we had changed our mind and were now going to the village of Ekwok. Ekwok was located about seven miles downriver. He said something else, but we weren't listening.

My friend climbed over his seat and began pulling cases of pop forward. Cans of pop were breaking open, and pop was spraying everywhere. I couldn't tell whether it was helping us or not because the airplane was flying fine at this point, as it had in cruise power on the way out to the village. We discussed going back to Dillingham to land on the long runway, but we were unwilling to face the music for what we had done. We decided to go on down the river to Ekwok. Ekwok had a longer runway then New Stuyahok, so we felt we could land there without using flaps.

We set up on a long final at Ekwok and announced our intentions on the radio as if nothing had happened. The first approach with no flaps was too fast. Rapidly running out of room without even touching down, I pushed the throttle against the firewall and went around, barely clearing the small trees at the end of the airport. Although we were heavy, we still had complete control of the airplane. We discussed planting it on the end and skidding to a stop with heavy brakes. I was doing most of the flying from the right seat; my injuries seemed insignificant at this point. On the next attempt to land, I planted the airplane on the end of the runway and jerked off the power.

My friend used the brakes heavily, but not so much that we were in danger of popping a tire. We came to a stop near the end of the airport, but in one piece. Now safely on the ground, we unloaded half of the aircraft.

Our mail agent had seen us land and came out to the airport, thinking that we had mail for him. We sheepishly explained to him the predicament we were in and how we had ended up in Ekwok. He said he didn't have a problem watching the mail for us while we made two trips to New Stuyahok.

At this point in the day, I decided that my leg didn't hurt that bad anymore, and I did the rest of the flying. We completed our mission and headed back to Dillingham. There wasn't any way for me to hide the fact that I hadn't landed at New Stuyahok with the original load of mail and that I had made two shuttles between Ekwok and New Stuyahok All that was left to explain was some of the more dramatic details.

I was immediately summoned to the chief pilot's office, where I was asked to explain several things, including why I would load the aircraft so far aft CG. My explanation about overhearing him and another pilot discussing that the more cargo you put in the back, the better it flew, didn't go over very well. The chief pilot demanded that I work a weight and balance out with him, so I tried my best to remember exactly how I had loaded the airplane.

At some point, the chief pilot threw up his hands and said something to the effect of, "There's not enough paper in this office to complete this weight and balance. My God, kid, what were you thinking?" He also had a few choice words to say about believing a couple of old-timers in casual conversation. I was sent home to think about how lucky I was to be alive, but instead of going home, I went out to the hangar and started working on my new snowmobile, which was in need of a little love.

It wasn't until I got home that night that I started feeling the fear I should've felt during the day. I started thinking that perhaps being a bush pilot wasn't for me. I kept making one stupid mistake after another, and every time I would miraculously survive. Every time I would promise myself and God that it would never happen again, but unfortunately, it would. I decided that it was time for me to stop pushing the envelope. I wasn't a test pilot; I was just a wannabe bush pilot. Perhaps it was time for me to face the fact that I was most likely never going to be as good as the pilots I idolized. I decided that I would be more diligent about using the radio, stop trying to be like the old-timers, and try even harder to make smart decisions in my life.

Looking back on that day, I will always believe that there was an angel controlling each wing. In my mind, there can be no other explanation for the airplane maneuvering the way it did under those circumstances. I spent the evening pacing back and forth across my living room. This time, my stupidity nearly killed a good friend of mine, and like always, it bothered me a lot. I was thanking God for allowing his guardian angels to gently redirect our flight path.

I promised God that if he would help me make better decisions, I would be a willing vessel for him to use at his discretion. All I could do was learn from my mistakes and pray that in the future, I would do better. Once again, I got down on my knees and gave my life to God, but it felt different this time. This time, it felt as though I really meant it.

I had heard that my dad was in negotiations to buy a single-engine deHavilland DHC-3 Otter. The one he was looking at had a 600-horsepower Pratt & Whitney R-1340 nine-cylinder air-cooled radial engine. It was a high-wing, propeller-driven, short-takeoff-and-landing aircraft and the big brother to the similar but smaller deHavilland DHC-2 Beaver. The Otter was about forty-one feet long with a wingspan of fifty-eight feet, and it was going to be configured for nine passengers. If I wanted a shot at flying that airplane, it was time to get my act together.

Present Day Dillingham

Chapter 23

TWO ANGELS AND A CASE OF BREAD

My dad finally purchased the deHavilland Otter he had been thinking about. Two of his pilots had experience in the Otter from previous jobs, so naturally they got checked out in the airplane first. By the time my dad got around to checking me out, it was deep into the fall. The Otter had been flown very hard that summer, and it was showing signs of fatigue.

The Otter normally had a steerable tail wheel that helped maneuver the aircraft on the runway in high winds. Unfortunately, this handy little asset was inoperative by the time I got checked out in the aircraft. My dad didn't want to spend the money to repair it, mostly because he believed it wasn't necessary.

The deeper we got into winter, the less interested the two pilots who were already checked out in the Otter became. The Otter ended up being the airplane I flew the most that winter. Despite the Otter needing a little love, I started to enjoy flying the airplane immensely. I was flying the Otter to and from all the nearby villages. The thing that bothered me the most about the airplane was that occasionally, just as I would touch down on landing, the rudder appeared to jam up. I would have to move the rudder in the opposite direction that I needed it to move before it would free up.

Most of the time when I would do this, it would appear as though I couldn't keep the airplane going straight because of my lack of ability. This bothered me to the point where I would complain about the rudder locking up on me to our chief mechanic. He would take the aircraft into the hangar and look it over. He would always come to the same conclusion: Lester sucks and should just learn to fly. I knew it wasn't right for the rudder to be locking up, but I also knew that they weren't going to fix it unless it was broken. I kept flying the airplane and would just be ready to make a quick jab in the opposite direction. That normally would free it back up, and it wouldn't give me any trouble for a while.

One day, I was unavailable to fly the Otter, so one of the other pilots who was already checked out in it took the trip. When he came back, he complained about several things, including the same rudder problem that I had been complaining about. He also made the comment, "I can't believe Lester's flying this hunk of junk." The mechanics took it back into the hangar and came to the same conclusion they had in the past. This time, they added a new name to the sucky pilot list.

The next day when I came to work, the Otter had been given a clean bill of health. I was told to go to Bethel and help move mail to some of Bethel's nearby villages. Bethel is 170 miles northwest of Dillingham and is the air-transportation hub for fifty-six villages in the Yukon-Kuskokwim Delta area. My dad had a base of operation in Bethel that operated a small fleet of Cessna 207s, affectionately called sleds. Yute Air pilots moved mail, freight, and passengers to all the surrounding villages, and occasionally they would get behind hauling the mail. When that happened, my dad would send me up north in the Otter to help get caught up.

I had a friend who liked going on road trips with me, so I called him up, and we were soon ready to head to Bethel. While trying to start the Otter without heating it up first, I backfired the engine, and it caught on fire. I grabbed a fire extinguisher out of the gas truck I was parked beside and promptly put the fire out. As it turns out, a dry chemical fire extinguisher makes a huge mess, and in my situation, the mechanics were happy to supervise my friend and I in cleaning it up. We finally got underway and arrived at Bethel just before dark. The Otter had a thick blanket that was designed to fit perfectly around the engine to keep it warm while on the ground. We carried the blanket with us everywhere we went.

We didn't have any way to heat the Otter up in the morning, and not wanting to burn up our only ride home attempting to start a cold engine again, my friend and I slept on the hangar floor and periodically throughout the night went outside, removed the blanket, and started the engine to warm it up.

Eager to get our work done and go home, at first light we loaded the Otter with mail. We flew all day to various villages and were making quite a dent in the enormous pile of bypass mail. The last load of the day was going to Napakiak, a little village less than ten miles from Bethel. When we arrived at Napakiak, we flew over the runway and entered a normal traffic pattern.

Less than ten feet before I touched the wheels on the ground, I pushed forward on both brake pedals to test the brakes. Just then, both brake pedals fell forward and jammed themselves between the firewall and the rudder pedals. I immediately added power, and with only aileron and elevator to control the airplane, I managed to get up to a comfortable altitude where I could let my friend fly while I tried to figure out what had happened.

As soon as I lay on my back and shimmied underneath the dashboard, I could see the problem. The brake pedals were attached to the rudder pedals. The brake pedals were also attached to a brake actuator by a short rod that activated the brake when the pedals were pushed forward. The bolts that attached the brake pedal to the actuator rod were supposed to be positioned in such a way that the bolt heads faced each other. Someone had positioned the bolts so that the threads faced each other. Over time, the bolts had hung up on one another enough that they had worn down to the point where they broke off at the same time, most likely when I pushed on both brakes to test them prior to touching down.

There weren't any tools or parts in the cockpit that I could use to hold the brake pedals upright where they belonged. I happen to glance into the back of the plane and noticed a case of bread on top of the load up near the cockpit door. In those days, bread bags were tied with wire coated with paper. I opened the case of bread and unwired twenty bags. I stripped the paper off the wires and made two separate pieces of wire out of the twenty wires by twisting ten wires together for each. I then went back under the dashboard and used the wires to wire the brake pedals back on to the actuator rod.

The wind wasn't blowing that day, and I landed without needing the brakes until the airplane was slow; at that point, I only used the brakes as I needed for taxiing. We unloaded our freight, and I crawled back underneath the dashboard again. Everything looked good, so I decided to take the airplane back to Bethel.

It was starting to get dark, and I had never flown the Otter after dark before, so we were in a big hurry to get airborne. It was only about ten miles back to Bethel. The weather had been fine all day in the Yukon-Kuskokwim. We took off to the north, expecting to make a gentle right turn and immediately spot Bethel. At about three hundred feet, we flew right into a snow squall.

The Otter was only equipped with a needle and a ball operated by an electric gyro to keep the airplane upright and coordinated in its turns. It had an NDB, but we weren't prepared to look up the NDB frequency, and we weren't familiar enough with the area to know what that frequency was. It was about then that I realized we didn't have any working lights in the cockpit. I wasn't very experienced at instrument flying, especially with only a needle and a ball, but I managed to keep the airplane upright and in a gentle turn to the right. As it turned out, the important instruments glowed in the dark, and we didn't need the lights after all.

We were only in the snow squall for a few minutes when my friend spotted Bethel straight ahead of us. We went on into Bethel, landed, and slept on the hangar floor one more night while periodically running our engine so that we could leave for home the next morning. When the time came, we loaded some freight that my dad wanted us to bring back to Dillingham. At the last minute, a snowmobile was brought out to us that we were told was a priority item.

The only place we could put the snowmobile was in the very back, so after loading it, we were a little heavy in the tail. It was a beautiful day, so we elected to fly low through the mountains. As we approached Togiak Lake, it was starting to get turbulent, so we climbed up to about two thousand feet. As we flew along, we started smelling gas, and within minutes the cockpit floor on the right side was wet and two puddles of gas had developed under the right seat rudder pedals. The engine was losing power, and we were no longer able to maintain altitude.

I made an announcement on the company frequency hoping that someone would answer. One of the company pilots answered back, and we told him about our situation. Togiak Lake was covered in snow, and we had no way of knowing how deep it was. We were out of options at this point and committed ourselves to land on the frozen lake full of snow. We touched down, and the weight in the tail kept us from tipping over as we landed in the deep snow. We might not have liked loading the snowmobile at the last minute in the tail of the airplane, but it sure did come in handy.

We sat there on the lake for about an hour before our Cessna 185 on wheel skis showed up with a mechanic. He soon figured out that a fuel line had come apart at a junction, and he fixed the problem in no time at all. The pilot of the 185 suggested we take off while he was still on the ground in case something went wrong.

I was surprised at how well the Otter handled in deep snow. Once we got the airplane moving, it climbed up on top of the snow like a floatplane getting on step. We took off without any problems and continued to Dillingham. As planned, when we arrived in Dillingham, I complained about the rudders jamming up again. I even gave the mechanics a hint. I said, "I think the problem might be in the rudder pedals themselves." I left what was left of the nuts, bolts, and washers in a pile beneath the rudder pedals for them to find.

The next day, when I showed up to fly the airplane, I climbed underneath the dashboard to see if the problem had been solved. This time, the bolts were orientated properly, and I never had any more trouble with my rudder jamming up. I flew the Otter the rest of that winter without any problems.

I was sent back up to Bethel several more times and learned a lot about flying in that area. The wind was the big problem for me because none of the strips had cross runways. What a lot of the villages did have, however, were lakes, rivers, or roads that worked just as well. All of the pilots who flew in the Bethel area were diligent about using the radio, and it helped me reinforce my commitment to the use of the radio every time I would fly in that area.

I think flying out of Bethel is where I made up my mind to join the movement that was taming Bristol Bay. I prayed a lot when I flew out of Bethel. It seemed like the harder I tried to be conservative, the more things would go wrong. I never lost my faith in God, and knowing that Joe was with me was enough to keep me out of trouble. I was trying hard to clean up my act, and it was finally working.

Chapter 24

THE BIGGER THE AIRPLANE, THE HARDER JOE'S JOB

My dad's company, Yute Air Alaska, was getting calls from clients needing larger-sized freight moved, so he purchased a Douglas DC-3. The DC-3 was bigger than any of his other airplanes, at about sixty-four feet long and a wingspan of ninety-five feet. It was pulled along by two Pratt & Whitney R-1830 1,200-horsepower piston engines. It cruised along at 207 miles per hour and could haul seven thousand pounds legally.

The seller delivered the airplane to Dillingham and stayed for the summer to get the DC-3 program off and running. He didn't plan to stay in Alaska for the winter, so my dad and I headed for Seattle to get our DC-3 type ratings. Any aircraft having a gross weight of more than 12,500 pounds required a special rating that was specific to that aircraft, called a type rating.

We arrived in Seattle on a Friday afternoon. We were looking forward to spending the weekend together before we started our training. We hadn't spent much time together for a while, and we were trying to think of something that we would both enjoy doing when we ran across an ad for skydiving. Neither one of us had ever been skydiving before. After discussing it over dinner, we decided to go for it.

The next morning, we called the skydiving company on the phone and made reservations for Sunday morning. We didn't have cell phones, so the only way for anyone to get a hold of us was to leave a message at the front desk of the hotel. Saturday night, when we returned to our hotel after touring Seattle all day, there was a message from my dad's sister insisting that we attend a barbecue on Sunday. Neither of us had seen his sister or her family in years, so we decided to blow off the skydiving and go to the barbecue.

Monday morning, we arrived at the flight school to begin our training and overheard the staff talking about a skydiving accident that had happened on Sunday. We soon put two and two together and realized it was the skydiving company and morning class that we had signed up for. The airplane had some type of a mechanical malfunction and all the students who were on board perished. I guess God still had a plan for my dad and I because he sure had our back on that one. My guardian angel Joe probably thought the worst thing he was going to have to deal with on our trip was keeping us from going down one of the many one-way streets that Seattle is famous for.

Thankful for the barbecue that had literally saved our lives, we eagerly began our training. The DC-3 was configured so that one of us could fly and the other could ride in the jump seat. We both did all the ground training together, and while we were learning the preflight, I started to argue with the instructor over, of all things, port and starboard. The instructor was trying to tell me that when you are standing in the cargo bay of the aircraft facing the tail, starboard was on the aircraft's left side and port was on the aircraft's right. He then went on to say if you are facing the cockpit, starboard was on the aircraft's right side and port was on the aircraft's left. This I agreed with; the other was utter nonsense.

My dad knew I was right, but being a practical man, he told

me in front of the instructor that I was thinking about boats; this was an aircraft, and things were different. He went on to say, "Let's just get through this and go home." I knew what he was trying to do was the right thing, so I kept my mouth shut, and soon we were in the flying stage of our training.

It was cloudy that day, and I don't think we were up as high as the instructor would've liked, but everything was going smoothly, so I think he made an exception when it came to the altitude required to practice stalls. I was the first one to try this maneuver. I had never done an approach to a stall before; I had always done full stalls. No one had explained to me the difference. so when I felt the buffet of the stall, I buried the flight controls back in my lap. The airplane broke off abruptly, with the left wing lower than the right.

I recovered the same way I had always recovered: I shoved the nose down, leveled the wings, and came in with max power calling for takeoff flaps. I thought the recovery went rather smoothly, but I was a little surprised at how much altitude we lost. The instructor was freaking out. I guess he didn't like the up-close-and-personal view he was getting of the residential district we were flying over. I think it shook him up because he called it a day. The next day we found ourselves back in ground school, covering approach to stalls and recovery. The rest of the training went well, and soon we were on our way to Alaska with our type ratings in the DC-3.

When we arrived back in Dillingham, the ink still wet on our certificates, we started watching for a trip that would help pay for my training. The former owner of the DC-3 agreed to stick around and help me get acquainted with flying it around Bristol Bay. The first trip to come up was a charter to Levelock, sixty miles east of Dillingham along the Kvichak River.

My instructor and I loaded up the cargo, and with me in the left seat, we headed for Levelock. My instructor had been to Levelock earlier in the summer, and I had been to Levelock on and off since I started flying commercially. In fact, I was sent to Levelock at the age of eighteen in a Cherokee Six to pick up a woman who had chartered Yute Air to transport her back to Dillingham. When I arrived, the woman took one look at me and told me I was too young to be a pilot. I replied by saying, "It doesn't take age to fly an airplane, lady. It takes talent." Not armed with the social skills required to convince the woman to climb aboard, I ended up flying back to Dillingham alone.

This time, I was flying to Levelock with an instructor who flew the DC-3 a bit recklessly, and although by now most everyone was using the radio, including myself, I was still flying like I believe the old bush pilots had flown. I guess what I'm trying to say is that neither one of us bothered to check NOTAMs (notices to airmen that would have included information about runway closures).

When we arrived at Levelock, we flew over the runway to look at the wind sock and determine which way to land. To our surprise, the main runway was closed because of some extensive maintenance that was going on. Back then, Levelock had a short cross runway, and thankfully, that runway was open. My instructor felt the cross strip was long enough, so we positioned ourselves for landing.

This was my first time landing the DC-3 with a load, and certainly my first landing on a short runway with the aircraft. I touched the main wheels down just past the end, and with heavy braking, stopped without running out of room. We unloaded the airplane and headed back to Dillingham. When we got back to Dillingham, the instructor told my dad, "Your kid landed on the cross strip at Levelock like he'd been doing it his whole life. I think my work here is done." The next day, my instructor said goodbye and left the state.

My dad called the FAA and asked them to send someone

down to give us both 135 check rides. The FAA man who showed up was well into his sixties. He was about five feet eight inches tall, with short white hair. He was of average build for a man his age and was dressed in work clothes much like the ones we were wearing. We immediately felt comfortable talking to the man. He was planning to fly to Costa Rica the following week to enjoy his golden years hanging out on the beach. He was easy to work with and very accommodating.

The oral consisted of an hour discussion about how cheap it was to live in Costa Rica. After we were thoroughly briefed on beachfront living, the man suggested that we all go up in the airplane at the same time. I was the first to fly, and after I completed the air work, the man asked me to leave the left seat. He instructed my dad to sit down.

When my dad finished his portion of the air work, the man told him to go wait in the back and called me back to the left seat. When I sat back down in the left seat, he asked me if I had an instructor rating.

I replied by saying, "Yes. I have a single-engine instructor rating."

The man said, "You're going to need a multiengine instructor rating eventually, so I'm going to give you a multiengine instructor check ride." He then ordered me out of the left seat, and he gracefully slipped over from the right seat to the left. I sat back down in the right seat not knowing what to expect.

The man said, "I'm going to do a right 360-degree steep turn, and you're going to teach me." He immediately started turning to the right, and as he turned, he was climbing. His climb got steeper and steeper, to the point where I begin to worry about him stalling the aircraft. I grabbed the controls and lowered the nose. The whole time he had been turning, I had been trying to talk him out of the steep climb verbally. All the man said was, "Next time, don't wait so long to grab the controls." He then ordered me out of the right seat, and as gracefully as he had moved over, he moved back. I sat back down in the left seat, and we finished our check rides.

My dad managed to find a lot of work for the airplane, and I was having a blast flying with him. My dad was having fun flying the old gooney bird himself, but he had a company to run, so he chose one of his mechanics who had a commercial instrument multiengine rating to be my copilot. The guy was a good mechanic, and my dad felt that it would be a good idea to have a mechanic along on some of the longer trips we were now starting to go on. I had fun flying with the guy, but I missed flying with my dad.

In the spring, my dad decided to spray-foam his entire hangar, so he told me to get the airplane ready to go to Anchorage. The plan was for me to fly to Anchorage, rent a U-Haul, pick up the barrels from the supplier, load them into the airplane, and bring them back to Dillingham. The plan had an adventurous sound to it, so I immediately started preparing for the trip.

The DC-3 burned 100 gallons of gas an hour and held 800 gallons, so we would have eight hours of fuel with full tanks. Round-trip fuel to Anchorage, going through Lake Clark Pass, would take about six hours, but I elected to fill up the tanks so I could do some sightseeing on the way in. I filled both tanks to the top and then went up to my dad's office to tell him that I was ready to go. As soon as I walked into his office, he told me that he had received an urgent call and I needed to take 1,500 gallons of gas to the nearby village of Manokotak immediately. Manokotak was only twenty miles west of Dillingham and had a 3,000-foot runway, more or less. The runway was in good condition year-round.

I told him that I had just put 800 gallons of gas in the DC-3 for the Anchorage flight. He basically said, in language I don't want to repeat, "Just take the 1,500 gallon of gas to Manokotak and then get into Anchorage and pick up my barrels of foam."

The way we hauled fuel in the DC-3 was to strap three 500-gallon tanks in the back; when we got to our destination, we used a standard one-inch water pump to pump out the gas. The water pump was gas-powered, and there weren't any flash arresters or other safety precautions in place. We just fired up the pump and hoped for the best.

I reluctantly put the tanks in the airplane, filled them with gas, and headed to Manokotak. When we arrived, we flew over the runway to look at the wind sock. I made the decision to land toward the south. We were heavier than I had ever flown the airplane, and this forced us to make an exceptionally wide pattern. We were on the radio the whole time announcing our position as we positioned ourselves to land to the south. We touched down on the end of the runway as slow as I was comfortable.

I left the flaps down full and push the nose over hard to increase drag. As the brakes began to heat up, they started getting soft. The brake pedals were slowly bleeding down and eventually bottomed out. They were still slowing us down, but I was thinking that if I were to release the brakes and build up hydraulic pressure, I would have even better brakes.

I was right about one thing: when I let up on the brakes, I could feel the hydraulic pressure building, and once the pressure built up, they felt hard. Unfortunately, when I tried to use them, they were ineffective. The heat had apparently glazed them over, and now we were without brakes. My angel Joe was probably sitting in the jump seat enjoying the ride until my feet came off the brakes. After that, I envision him outside the airplane pushing back on the nose, trying to keep us from ending up in the tundra.

My copilot was demanding that I put down the tail, but I

was afraid that if I did, I wouldn't be slowing down anymore. I chose to ignore him and keep the tail high in the air. I could feel the airplane slowing down, but I could also tell that we weren't going to stop in time. Just before we went off the end, I pulled the tail down and plowed right through the wooden runway end identifier.

There was a three-wheeler trail that went off the end of the runway and down to the tundra. The trail was well used and, for the first forty feet, as wide as the DC-3 wheelbase. We weren't going very fast at that point and only went off the end by about 30 feet before we stopped. Plowing through the wooden sign had put a small dent in the bottom of the wing and flap, but there was no structural damage.

The 1,500 gallons of gas had to be pumped off before we could attempt to pull the airplane back up onto the airport, so while the gas was being pumped off, I hitched a ride into the village on a three-wheeler to call my dad. The safest way to pull the DC-3 back up onto the airport was to use the tow bar that attached to the tail wheel. Unfortunately, the tow bar was back in Dillingham. The only airplane in Dillingham large enough to transport the tow bar was an aircraft called the Evangel.

he Evangel was an American twin-engine, tail-wheel-configuration, retractable-gear, light-passenger/cargo monoplane built by the Evangel Aircraft Corporation particularly for use by missionary groups in south America. The Evangel 4500-300 was built in Orange City, Iowa. Only a total of eight were ever completed.

My dad purchased one of the Evangels in the early '70s. He purchased the first one completed, N4501L. My dad's company eventually outgrew the Evangel, and he replaced it with a Navajo

Chieftain. I purchased the Evangel from him to transport nets and supplies in support of my fishing business.

Evangel

TMy dad soon showed up in my Evangel with the tow bar. By now, we had emptied the airplane and were ready to tow it back up onto the airport. By the time my dad showed up, the wind had switched directions and was blowing 180 degrees different than the direction it was blowing when we landed. Immediately, my dad jumped to the conclusion that we had landed with a tail wind, and without asking any questions, just started right in on one of his Phil Attacks. One of the locals who had witnessed the whole thing finally convinced my dad that we had in fact landed into the wind, and that the wind had switched after we landed.

My dad eventually stopped frothing at the mouth and flicking his false teeth long enough for us to get the DC-3 backed up onto the runway and head to Dillingham, where we removed the three 500-gallon tanks and continued our trip to Anchorage. My guardian angel Joe was probably hoping big airplanes would make his job a lot easier, but what he found out was, the bigger the airplane, the harder his job.

Chapter 25

LIGHT FROM ANGELS CAN SHINE THROUGH A BLIZZARD

My dad stayed busy running the air taxi, but occasionally, when he felt it was necessary, he would fly as my copilot. My dad didn't always trust me to push things as far as he would while getting the job done—mostly because he could tell I was trying to be conservative and not make so many mistakes. My dad would get the job done no matter what it took.

I remember landing at Ekwok with a thirty-knot crosswind, and the right flap failed feet above the ground. The crosswind was from the right, so the failure worked with us more than against. We used vise grips to clamp the flap into place and flew home after using an electric drill to run our fuel pump to get the engines started.

One trip he felt it necessary to fly with me on was in the middle of the winter to the small village of Tununak. He called me into work early one morning to get the DC-3 ready for an important mission. He told me that a village on the edge of Etolin Strait, 120 miles west of Bethel, had lost its only generator, and the village was without the electricity needed for lights and running their electrically operated oil-burning stoves for heating. Heating with wood was not as common in Tununak as it was in other villages because of the lack of firewood in the area.

The only building with electricity and heat was the school, which had its own emergency generator. The entire village population was depending on the school for food and shelter. The new generator was to be flown to us from Anchorage in a DC-6 that morning, and we were to transport it in our DC-3 to Tununak. The village had been without power for two days. To make things worse, the nastiest storm of the year had moved into the west coast of Alaska, and it didn't look like it was going anywhere anytime soon. No one was flying, but given the importance of the mission, my dad decided to, in his words, "Go look." I knew from past experiences that this meant that we were going to take the village their generator.

When the generator arrived and we got a look at it, I couldn't see how it was going to fit into the DC-3, but my dad remained optimistic. The generator itself weighed six thousand pounds—practically the total capacity of the DC-3. It was quite a struggle getting it on board, but with the use of a front-end loader and lots of dunnage, we finally got the generator in the DC-3 and strapped down.

I remember standing back away from the airplane and observing that the fuselage looked a lot like a banana. I pointed this out to my dad, but he insisted that it looked fine, so we gassed the airplane and pushed on with our mission. The DC-3 had been updated with a Loran-C navigation system. I was familiar with the Loran because I had one in my boat. The Loran in the DC-3 wasn't user-friendly, but I was familiar with its basic functions.

We departed Dillingham and, with the use of the Loran, went directly to the village of Toksook. Toksook and Tununak are separated by a peninsula of land and are approximately five miles from each other. The Loran had a limited database that didn't include Tununak but thankfully did have Toksook. My dad was familiar with the area because he had been flying the west coast of Alaska most of his adult life. He knew that in the winter, there was a snowmobile trail that went from Toksook to Tununak, and he was hoping that the ceiling was high enough that we could at least see straight down and follow the snowmobile trail. Without electricity, the phones were out in Tununak, and there was no communication directly with the village.

Toksook had working phones. By calling Toksook, we got a secondhand weather report for Tununak because Toksook was in contact with Tununak by radio. The report that we got for Tununak indicated the winds were out of the south at more than forty knots directly down the runway, but the visibility was a quarter mile. My dad told me that the visibility from the air would be better than the visibility on the ground, and he felt that if we were to get lined up with the runway, we could land even with the limited visibility.

The snowmobile trail went up and over the 338-foot-high terrain that separated the two villages. The end of the Tununak runway was literally right on the coast of Etolin Strait; a narrow strip of sandy beach was the only thing between the water and the airport. Of course, this time of year, the sand had been replaced with sea ice. The airport and village both were in a small cove lined with cliffs that on a good day would hardly be noticeable. On a bad day, feet off the ground, just knowing they were there was concerning.

As we approached the village of Toksook, we descended as low as we safely could. My dad instructed me to fly the airplane and leave the looking outside to him. I did what I was told and flew directly over the village—and sure enough, my dad could see the trail. He gave me headings to fly that took us up and over the low-lying terrain and directly over the Tununak airfield. He told me he could see as well as he had hoped, and he gave me a heading to fly that would take us out to sea.

My dad told me to descend and stopped me at about five hundred feet above the ice. He instructed me to turn 90 degrees to the right and then immediately back to the left 270 degrees. We ended up on the reciprocal heading that had taken us out to sea. The salt water was completely frozen over and hard to see, but my dad could see pressure ridges and enough jagged ice chunks that he was comfortable with our altitude.

Once inbound, we were facing into the strong wind, and it was helping us maintain a slower than normal ground speed. The Loran could have been used to navigate to the airport, but we had neglected to save our position as we flew over the Tununak airport, so at this point the Loran wasn't going to be much help. My dad's plan was for us to see the shoreline in time to either land on the runway or make a turn and escape back out to sea. His general plan seemed reasonable; the execution was a little less refined.

This mission was of the utmost importance, and my dad was willing to spend time poking around for the runway. I was thinking that if we were to get close enough to the shore, I could put a waypoint in the Loran so we would at least know where the shore was. The way we were doing it, we didn't have any way of knowing how close to the shore we were getting.

Once we were heading inbound, we descended even further to about three hundred feet above the ice and put the landing gear down. The Loran was indicating that we were traveling at about seventy miles per hour over the ground. Suddenly, a large dark crack in the ice appeared in front of us. At first, we were startled, thinking that it might be an indication that the shore was nearby. Then we realized that the crack in the ice was heading in the same direction we were. It was the only thing my dad had seen clearly for quite some time, and he told me to follow it.

I strained to see out the front window. I turned my head from side to side to follow the crack and at the same time prepare myself for an escape if needed—a type of flying I called rubbernecking. I got down even lower, straining my eyes to see through the blowing snow. I put the flaps down and slowed even more. The wind was howling, but it was blowing straight offshore, and even though it was turbulent and reducing the visibility, it was probably the best thing we had going for us at the time.

As it turned out, the crack in the ice led us directly to the end of the runway. In fact, the first thing we spotted before anything else was the wooden structures that marked the end of the runway. I planted the main wheels just past the wooden runway end identifier and dug deep into the brakes.

We couldn't have been going more than forty miles per hour over the ground when we touched down, and with our tail high in the air, praying we were lined up, we stopped in no more than three airplane links. We just sat there in the middle of the runway. I'm not sure what my dad was doing at the time, but I was thanking God for the solid ground underneath our wheels and the crack in the ice that led us to the end of the runway.

We sat there not knowing exactly what to do. The blowing snow was so thick we couldn't see the sides of the runway. We were sure we were on the runway but not sure where the ramp was. From experience, my dad knew it was up ahead of us on the left somewhere. We finally decided to creep ahead and see if we could possibly find it.

As we started to creep forward, a snowmobile appeared out of the blowing snow. It was heading straight for us. We stopped, and the snowmobile turned around directly in front of us and started slowly moving forward. We could tell that he was leading us somewhere, so we followed the taillights until we reached the ramp. The taxiway for the ramp was in the shape of a horseshoe, so we only had to make a slight left turn to get off the runway. This worked in our favor. We could've just stopped on the runway, but my dad didn't think the runway was wide enough for us to unload the generator, so I'm glad that we were led to an area with more room to unload.

We weren't thinking about taking back off at the time, but from where we were parked, all we had to do was make a slight turn to the right, and we would be back on the runway. We shut the engines off and made our way to the back of the plane. Both of us were pushing on the door, trying to open it against the wind. The man who had led us in on his snowmobile was also helping us open the door, and between the three of us we managed to open it and strap it in place with a cargo strap so the door wouldn't slam shut on someone by accident.

We left the main cargo door shut and signaled to the man to come on board because communicating in the blizzard would be impossible. We hooked up a ladder for the man to climb up. Inside, the man pulled back the hood to his parka and revealed his face. He was about five feet four inches tall. He was dressed from head to foot in garments made from caribou hide. The ring around the hood of his parka was made of wolf. The man had shoulder-length black hair with a straggly beard and a mustache full of ice crystals. His face was weathered, and he appeared to be in his early forties.

We introduced ourselves, and he told us is name was Joe. He gave us his last name, but I couldn't begin to pronounce it. He was a Yupik Eskimo and spoke broken English. There was a river that ran by the village that dumped out into Etlin Straight not far from the airport. Joe told us that he was down by the river gathering ice to melt for drinking water and thought he might have heard an airplane fly over him, but he couldn't see anything. Around the same time, he thought he heard an airplane and heard the ice split. He said that sometimes during heavy offshore winds, cracks in the ice appear, exposing new hunting opportunities. He was starting to explore the crack just as we flew over and landed on the airport.

The whole village had been expecting us to come, but not today. Joe had a radio with him and used it to call someone in the village. We could hear him communicating with someone in Yupik, but we weren't sure what was being said.

When Joe was finished speaking to the voice on the other end of the radio, he told us that he was having to argue about our being at the airport. He also said that the equipment they intended to unload us with hadn't been started in several days and most likely wouldn't start now. Joe said he had a trick or two up his sleeve and assured us the equipment would be at the airport as soon as possible. He said goodbye to us and bundled back up in his furs.

We watched from the door as his taillights disappeared into the blizzard. We never doubted Joe for a minute, and sure enough, it wasn't long before a small group of people with the necessary equipment showed up to unload their generator. We never saw Joe again, and even though I didn't think of it at the time, I now believe that my guardian angel Joe once again made an appearance to assist us in our time of need. If it wasn't my guardian angel, I'm grateful for the man who showed up out of nowhere and directed us to a safe place to unload, and then organized an unloading party in freezing temperatures, high wind, and blizzard conditions in record time.

After everyone left, we started our engines and gingerly made our way to the airport. We were surprised to see bright lights positioned on both sides of the airport, clearly marking the edge of the runway and making it safer for us to take off. We took off toward the high terrain, and I stayed on the instruments, climbing out as steep as I dared while my dad watched for clues on the ground to guide me either left or right as needed until we were high enough to clear all the terrain in our area. We used the Loran to go directly to Bethel. When we arrived at Bethel, curious as to how much gas remained, I checked the tanks. I had only seen tanks this dry once before. I knew exactly who was responsible for helping us pull off our rescue mission, and while I waited for the fuel truck to arrive, I thanked God for cracking the ice and sending his guardian angels to protect us while we helped to restore power to a village in need.

I have never been back to Tununak, but will never forget the experience and will always be grateful for what I believe was angels lining the airport with their light so we could stay safely lined up as we took off from Tununak Airport in one of the worse blizzards I have ever been outside in.

Chapter 26

JOE KNOWS BEST

A few winters after our rescue mission, I had a near-death experience in the DC-3 while trying to leave Dillingham for Anchorage. It was one of those early spring days when the temperature rose above freezing during the day and dipped below freezing toward the afternoon. One of my friends wanted me to instruct him in his Super Cub on skis. We had been planning it for a while, and for one reason or another, I kept putting him off. The latest reason was that Bristol Bay had been plagued with a severe ice storm, but we were finally getting a break in the weather.

I got up early to help my friend get his airplane warmed up and all the snow and ice cleaned off. The weather had been so bad the last couple weeks that his Super Cub was covered in ice and snow. We tried to clean it off when we first met at his aircraft in the morning, but the ice wasn't coming off. We were afraid we were going to damage the airplane if we kept trying to remove the ice, so we decided to wait.

The weather was forecasted to warm up during the day, so I stayed busy doing chores around the house. When the temperature came up above freezing, we met back at the airplane to remove the remainder of the ice. Before we went flying, I went back to my house to pick up my camera. My parents had gone into Anchorage for business, so they hadn't been home for about a week. When I ran into the house to grab my camera, I noticed a message flashing on my answering machine. The message was from my dad. He wanted me to load some crated airplane engines into the DC-3 and bring them into Anchorage so he could ship them out to be rebuilt.

I couldn't remember talking to him about getting the engines into Anchorage, so I dismissed the whole thing as an idea he came up with while sitting in Anchorage with nothing to do. I had canceled flying with my friend so many times, I wasn't going to cancel again. I ignored the message and met up with my friend to go flying.

We were gone for at least three hours. When I got home, I noticed another message. It was from my dad. This time, the message was more of a demand for me to bring his engines into Anchorage rather than a request. He was using colorful language, and I could hear his false teeth clicking around in his mouth as he threatened to fire me if I didn't show up in Anchorage that night. He even went so far as to say that he was going to disown me.

I decided I'd better take his engines into Anchorage before he had a major meltdown. I went to the airport to see what shape the DC-3 was in, and as I expected, it was a real mess. No one had deicing fluid in Dillingham back then, so all the snow and ice had to be removed with a broom. The DC-3 might fly like a Super Cub, but whenever you loaded the aircraft and tried to sweep the snow from the wing stabilizers and control surfaces, you got a feel for how big it really was.

I decided I was going to have to recruit some help if I had any chance of cleaning off the snow and ice. I called my cousin who lived close to the airport and asked him if he wanted to go on a road trip with me to Anchorage. He was excited for the opportunity and said he was on his way to the airport. My cousin wasn't a pilot, so I needed to round up a copilot to fly with me.

I called an uncle who had flown with me a few times before and asked him if he would like to go with me. He must've known more about the mission than he let on because he didn't hesitate in saying no. I told him about the first message that my dad had left on my recorder. He said, "Don't worry about your dad. He just has too much time on his hands. Let's just wait until tomorrow, and we will clean the airplane off during the day." What he said reinforced my first impression, but he hadn't heard the second message. He went on to say that it was already getting too late in the afternoon to clean off the airplane and go to Anchorage.

I didn't tell him about the second message; I just said, "Thanks. I'll talk to you tomorrow." I knew I could always count on my friend who was nearly killed in the Islander with me, so I gave him a call. He said that he was always up for a road trip, and before long, I had my cleaning crew at the airport. I was busy strategically placing heaters and hoses to heat the engines when they arrived, so I sent them out onto the wings with brooms to get started. When I was finished with the heaters, I joined them on the wings.

We decided to get most of the snow and ice off the wings and assess the situation after that. We worked for two hours and got the wings and the horizontal stabilizer as clean as we could, but there was still snow and ice adhering to the wing stabilizers and control surfaces that we just couldn't get off. The top of the airplane had a foot of snow with ice underneath down its entire length. We tried to clean it off, but we didn't have anything to reach that high, so we convinced ourselves that it would blow off as we accelerated down the runway.

Frustrated and tired, I began to think being fired and disowned was a bargain compared to trying to get all the ice off the gooney bird. We decided that it was impossible to clean the airplane off and made plans to meet back at the airplane in the morning. Before we left we, we decided to load the engines so that there would be one less thing to do in the morning. The engines were in large crates that we couldn't double-stack, so to get all the crates in the airplane, we ended up a little over the limits of aft CG. After loading the airplane, I went home exhausted from the day's events.

When I got home, there was another message waiting for me. I contemplated whether I should even listen to it. I finally gave in and listened to the message, and by the tone of his voice and the clicking of his false teeth, it was obvious that he was past the Phil Attack stage and into a complete meltdown. He had obviously had some time to think about his previous threats and had decided that the punishment he had previously mentioned wasn't going to be harsh enough, so he had added the promise to make my life a living purgatory if I didn't get his engines into Anchorage that night.

Not wanting to be without a job and family, and certainly not wanting to live my life in living purgatory, I decided that it was in my best interest to get his engines into Anchorage. I was unsure whether the airplane was going to fly in the condition that it was in, but I was starting to have a Phil Attack of my own and was willing take the risk just to shut him up. I didn't think there was much more we could do about cleaning off the airplane, but I rallied the crew and told them I was confident that if we were to scrape just a little more ice off the wings and horizontal stabilizer, it would fly.

It was already dark by now, and we put in another hour trying to clean the ice off the airplane. We decided that it was as good as it was going to get, so we pulled the blankets off the engines and climbed into the airplane, determined to get to Anchorage.

While the plane's engines were warming up, I filed an instrument flight plan. We completed our run-up, picked up our clearance, and taxied for the end of runway 01. I'm not sure why I chose runway 01; looking back, I'm sure Joe was behind that decision.

It was dark, cold, and foggy, and even though all the signs were pointing toward blowing the whole thing off and going home, I was focused on getting off the ground and heading for Anchorage. I should have known my dad wouldn't have followed through with his threats. As soon as he got his engines, the next day he would have forgotten about the whole thing. Joe was doing everything but hitting me over the head to stop me from attempting the takeoff, including this last development of un-forecasted fog that had rolled in. Ignoring all the signs, I was determined that nothing was going to deter me from completing the mission. I gave my copilot a last-minute briefing and set the power to max takeoff.

My copilot was monitoring the engine instruments to make sure that we didn't over-boost the engines. The tail came up where I thought it should, and I started to relax. I forced the airplane to stay on the ground to build up extra speed before lifting off. When I finally let the airplane fly, it was slowly rolling to the left as it gained altitude. I tried to compensate with the right aileron and rudder, but it wasn't working. When I ran out of aileron, I did the only thing I felt I had left to do: I pulled the right throttle back abruptly. When I did that, the right wing came down—but so did the airplane.

We touched down on the airport at about a hundred miles per hour with only five hundred feet of runway remaining. Out of the corner of my eye, I could see that my copilot had decided to put his head between his legs in the crash position. I'm not sure where he learned that from, but it wasn't from me. I was taught not to ever quit flying until the airplane was in the chocks and tied down. He was no longer monitoring the engine instruments as I pushed up the throttles. I knew I was over-boosting the engine, but I wasn't going to crash with two good engines. Besides, stopping was out of the question at this point.

We lifted off again for the second time, and again the airplane was rolling to the left—this time not as violently, but I soon ran out of rudder and aileron. At this point, I took advantage of the eight hundred feet of tundra that was between the end of the runway and the trees. I jerked the right throttle off, and the airplane settled gently down onto the tundra at over a hundred miles per hour. I closed the left throttle, and because the landing lights were so bright, I could watch as the trees rapidly approached the front window. Amazingly, it felt like we were landing on skis. The tail was high in the air, and the landing lights were illuminating the area where we were going to end up.

I noticed a fifty-foot-wide void in the trees just off to my left. I immediately went into preservation mode and decided to try to put the nose of the airplane in the area with no trees. Just as I added power to the right engine, hoping to track left, we struck a tree with the right wing, and it pulled us around. The next thing I knew, we were stopped on the edge of the tree line with the engines still running. Out of the cockpit window, all we could see were trees. The plane was sitting there like we were back at parking.

We were all pretty freaked out at this point. We unbuckled our belts and ran toward the rear of the plane. As I was running, I realized the engines were still on. I ran back up to the cockpit and firmly pulled the mixtures back, cutting my thumb on something in the process. I managed to turn the battery off before running to the back to meet up with my friends.

Once outside, I noticed that my friend and cousin were running back toward the airport. I'm not sure why, but it seemed like a good idea, so I ran after them. We got about two hundred feet from the airplane before falling into a creek we had opened with our main gear upon impact with the ground. I guess it wasn't the gentle landing I thought it was. The cold water must have brought us out of shock because after climbing out of the creek, we finally all just stopped.

As we looked back at the airplane, it didn't appear as though it had any damage. We ran around the airplane looking for visible damage. The right wingtip was missing, and we found it in a nearby tree. The wingtip was the only damage we could see while wading in two feet of snow. Not wanting to do any further damage to the airplane, we elected to put the control locks on before leaving. As we put them on, one of the metal hooks on the end of the bungee cord that was attached to the control lock somehow got stuck up in my right nostril.

I pulled the metal hook out of my nose, and blood started pouring down the front of my jacket. As I was standing in the woods with my thumb bleeding and blood all over my face and down my jacket, we heard my friend's dad yelling for us from the road. He was asking us if we were all okay. "Yes!" we answered enthusiastically. Once the control locks were in place, we ran toward the sound of his voice.

He was waiting for us up on the road with his truck. By this time, there were ambulances, fire trucks, and a whole crew of emergency personnel at the end of the runway. My friend's dad had watched us take off and drove five hundred feet from where we ended up. Knowing that we needed to check in with the emergency crews, we asked my friend's dad to drive us to the end of the airport where all the commotion was. There weren't any fences to prevent us from driving onto the runway, so my friend's dad drove us down to the end of the runway where the ambulance was waiting.

We checked in with the emergency crew and assured them that we were all okay. It was a little harder to convince the EMTs that I was okay with blood all over my face and down my front. One of the emergency personnel instructed us to get into the ambulance to get our blood drawn. I was deathly afraid of needles; besides, I wasn't sure if I had any extra blood to give at this point. I slipped into the crowd to try to get away. I spotted an uncle and asked him to get me out of there and take me home.

Eager to get the whole story firsthand, he gladly drove me home. I don't know how the other two guys left the scene, but I guess I figured at that point it was every man for himself. The next day, the local newspaper headline accused us of attempting to take off with our control locks on. The FAA had another theory: they find me $500 for attempting to take off with snow and ice adhering to the wing stabilizers and control surfaces. That was an assumption I was not able to argue with. I get my bullheadedness from my dad, and when I get something in my mind, I have a hard time shaking it. Thankfully, my guardian angel Joe is levelheaded, and even after I ignored all the road-closure signs he planted in my way, he still found a way to stop me. If Joel hadn't blocked all thoughts associated with using runway 19, heading toward the water, I'm certain this story would have a different ending, and it wouldn't be told by me.

I have been truly blessed throughout my life—given chance after chance to wise up. My dad denied any involvement in the accident, by the way. Using the argument that I was the pilot in command, he told me that I should never have let myself be coerced into doing anything that I knew to be wrong. How do you argue with logic like that? I paid for the damages out of my commercial fishing money the next summer. It was a lot more than the $500 I paid the FAA. I never bothered to argue with the newspaper about the control locks. I figured, what's the difference? I would have ended up in the same ditch either way.

Present Day Kanakanak Hospital

Chapter 27

JOE WILL NEVER LEAVE MY SIDE

I'd been flying for Yute Air for about ten years and had accumulated around ten thousand hours of flying air taxi when Yute Air got shut down for some of the shady operating practices that were becoming routine. The shutdown started out as a three-month suspension. The idea behind the suspension was to give Yute Air time to get its operating practices back in check. It was a reasonable request by FAA that my dad should have taken advantage of, but instead, true to his personality, he told the FAA to get off his property. He made some other threats and statements, and as a result, the suspension turned into a revocation of his operating certificate.

I was out commercial fishing at the time, and when I got back, I was out of a job. My dad went to court, but in the end, the ruling was that the certificate would be given back but my dad could only be a silent owner of the company; he couldn't hold any management position. He accepted the ruling and promptly sold Yute Air to three of its employees.

My dad soon started a new company called Fresh Water Adventures that consisted of one Grumman Goose and one employee. I moved to Anchorage and stayed busy flight-instructing.

Transitioning from the bush to the big city made me feel completely out of my element. I rented an apartment and put an ad in the newspaper offering to instruct individuals in their own aircraft. Surprisingly, I was instantly busy and flying almost every day.

I instructed in all types of aircraft—most of them taildraggers. My first student was in a J3 Cub with an upgraded engine that put out 115 horsepower. It had some other modifications that made it perform closer to a Super Cub than a J3. On our first flight, the student started feeling sick and informed me that he was going to throw up. I spent the next three minutes creatively instructing my new student how to puke out the window of a J3 Cub in the air without getting any on the instructor. It was time well spent, considering that it wasn't the only time this student used this procedure throughout his training.

During the winter, I had a student show up in a 1952 Cessna 170B with a 145-horsepower engine. It was in excellent condition— twenty-four feet long with a thirty-six-foot wingspan—and I thoroughly enjoyed teaching him to fly in it. At about twenty-five hours of instruction, the student hit a plateau of learning that affected his landings; they were inconsistent. One day, we would go out and he would land perfectly, and I would think, *Tomorrow is the day I'm going to solo him*. However, the next day we would go up for a final evaluation flight, and it was as if he was several lessons away from soloing.

The student felt that he was ready to solo and convinced me that it was his airplane, and if he wrecked it, it wouldn't be my responsibility. Reluctantly, I agreed to let him solo, but not until one final evaluation flight. I met him at the airport the next day, and on our preflight, we noticed that one of his position lights wasn't working. I had a toolbox in the Jeep I was driving, and by standing on the bumper of the Jeep, we fixed the light. After fixing the light, we went up for another session of stop-and-goes.

Stop-and-goes are exactly what they sound like. The pilot lands on the runway and comes to a complete stop before taking back off. This is different from a touch-and-go, where the pilot lands and then takes back off before coming to a complete stop. The stop-and-go is required for conventional-gear-type aircraft on the first solo flight. The student was flying flawlessly that day, and I felt good about letting him solo. I had him bring me back to the Jeep and drop me off, and then I instructed him to only make three stop-and-goes.

I stood by the Jeep as the student taxied the aircraft to the end of the runway and took off. The takeoff was flawless, and I was very encouraged with what I was seeing. I paid close attention to his landing, which was also flawless. I began to think that maybe I was being over-conscientious and that he was ready to solo after all.

The problems had always been his landings—not anything he was doing in the air—so I felt confident that even if something were to go wrong, he wouldn't hurt himself—only the aircraft. He took off for his second stop-and-go, and again, it was flawless. I watched him in the pattern as he came around for another landing. Again, the landing was perfect, and by now I was totally confident that I had made the right decision.

As he took off for the third and final landing, a friend of mine pulled up in his truck. I stood at his window speaking to him as my student went around for his third and final landing. Another aircraft showed up in the traffic pattern, and I could see that my student was going to extend downwind and give him room to land first. As I stood there talking to my friend, I started wondering how far away from the airport he had gone because I had lost sight of him. Knowing that he had never demonstrated any type of shortcomings in the air, I gave the situation the benefit of the doubt and continued to speak with my friend.

Suddenly, the Jeep that I had driven to the airport lunged forward, running over my toolbox with a loud crashing noise as my tools spilled out onto the ground. For an instant, I thought someone was stealing my Jeep. The Jeep immediately backed over the toolbox again with the same loud noise, as more tools splashed out onto the ground. I was running toward the Jeep but afraid to get either in front of or behind the Jeep lest I get run over.

As I approached the right side of the Jeep, I could see that it was my student at the wheel. I opened the door and jumped in, not wanting to be hurt by what appeared to be erratic behavior. The student put the Jeep in forward and this time ran over my toolbox with both front and rear tires. It appeared to me that he was fleeing the scene. Confused, I asked the student, "What's going on, and where is your airplane?"

He replied by stating that he had messed up bad this time. I told him that he appeared to be okay and that everything else could be fixed. I told him that we couldn't flee the scene. We were going to have to go back to the accident, if that was possible.

He turned and drove out onto the airport, and I could clearly see the airplane in the middle of the runway, upside down. When we arrived at the airplane, I made sure to get the keys out of the Jeep, and I tried to calm my student down. I told him that when the authorities came, that we had done nothing wrong; it was a simple accident, and it happens all the time. No one was hurt, and we would deal with the consequences together.

Gas was running out of the tanks onto the runway, and there were already several people there who had been attending a civil air patrol meeting. I recognized most of the people who were there because I had also attended several civil air patrol meetings. One of the men came up to me and described what he had witnessed. He said that the airplane landed and made a sharp right turn, followed by a sharp left turn, and then the airplane flipped over onto its back. The pilot jumped out and ran. He went on to say that he had to crawl into the aircraft and shut off the battery switch in fear that the plane might catch fire because of all the gas.

At this point, I was pretty much caught up on the events of the accident, having experienced the tight weaving back and forth on landing myself with this student. By now, there were a dozen civil air patrol individuals standing around the airplane. One of the older gentlemen took charge of the situation. It wasn't someone I had seen before, but he had a name I was familiar with, especially in situations like this one. Joe ordered one of the men to go and get a rope. While the man was gone, the airport manager showed up and immediately started to threaten that he was going to get a front-end loader and push the aircraft off the runway. He said this time of evening, airplanes would be coming back to the airport, and he couldn't have the airport closed in, fearing that some of the aircraft might be low on fuel.

Joe pulled me aside and told me not to worry about the airport manager. He said the airport manager wasn't going to push the aircraft off into the ditch. He assured me that he had done this type of rescue before, and it was no big deal.

Of course, I was flashing back to another Joe who had gotten me out of a similar jam in the past, and I was totally confident that this Joe was going to handle the situation with the same dominant approach. When the rope showed up, it was tied to the tail wheel. The rope was running up past the engine and down the runway. Once again, a man named Joe had organized a tug-of-war situation with an aircraft. Pleased with what I was seeing, I stood beside Joe as he gave the order for the rope to be pulled.

The result wasn't exactly what I had envisioned. The fuselage buckled about three feet forward of the horizontal stabilizer. The horizontal and vertical stabilizer ended up sitting on the top of the fuselage, pointing in the opposite direction than normal. Joe immediately told me not to worry. Apparently, there had been some fuselage damage already that wasn't apparent before we played tug-of-war with the aircraft. Joe suggested we tie the rope around the fuselage rather than onto the tail wheel.

We pulled the tail section back off the fuselage and back into its original location, give or take. After tying the rope around the fuselage, Joe ordered everyone to pull on the rope again. This time, the airplane flipped over to where it belonged, and the vertical and horizontal stabilizers stayed intact. Not wanting to risk pulling the tail section completely off the aircraft, I suggested that we rig up a harness and pull the aircraft from the two-main landing gear. This was an area I was familiar with, and my commercial fishing skills came into play rigging up the harness.

After the harness was in place, the police showed up and wanted to see the identification of everyone who was involved in the accident. I informed the police that we were going to be compliant with all their demands but we would like to get the airplane off the runway first because by then, there were airplanes circling overhead that needed to land. The police agreed.

I had my student walk beside the tail and help keep it going in the right direction as I pulled the airplane back to parking with the Jeep. We complied with all the paperwork, and the student thanked me for everything I had done. He told me that when the repairs were completed, he would give me a call. I never heard from him again.

It wasn't long after that incident that my dad asked me if I would be willing to sell out of the fishery and invest in his company. I had missed working with my dad, and the commercial salmon fishery in Bristol Bay had made a major downswing in the price per pound, so it didn't take me very long to decide to sell out of the fishery and join my dad. His new company only operated in the summer and primarily provided air transportation to people needing to fly to locations along the Nushagak River or north of Dillingham into the 4.2-million-acre Tikchik State Park and west into the 6.4-million-acre Togiak National Wildlife Refuge. His clients would choose to be either led by guides who were starting companies within Bristol Bay or do an independent adventure.

His business had quickly expanded past what he could handle with the one Goose, so I bought a Grumman Widgeon and signed on as a partner. I purchased the Widgeon in the middle of the winter and got it on the Fresh Water Adventures operating certificate in time for the upcoming season. I had a single-engine sea rating but not a multiengine sea, so my dad got into the Widgeon with me and we flew to Big Lake, a populated lake about thirty miles to the north of Anchorage, to begin my training.

I flew the airplane above the lake for a while, getting used to it before attempting my first landing. The Widgeon didn't have any controls on the right side, so I was depending on my dad to give me verbal advice as I learned how the aircraft handled on the water. Big Lake had about thirteen square miles of water, but it wasn't exactly round, and it had numerous islands.

I lined myself up on a reasonably long straight stretch and gently set the hull of the Widgeon down on the lake. The touchdown was smooth, but I didn't apply enough back pressure, and more of the nose area ended up on the water than I wanted. When this happens, the surface friction of the nose on the water will feel like the nose is sticking to the water. This feeling is associated with a louder than usual sound, and my first reaction was to pull back on the control wheel. When I did, it felt like the nose went too far in the air, so I shoved the nose back down. By now, the airplane was going slower, so when the nose met the water, the water repelled the nose, and we were in a porpoise— which is nothing more than a pilot-induced oscillation. It is called a porpoise because the airplane is mimicking an actual porpoise, only without any of the gracefulness.

I didn't know exactly how to get out of it, so I asked my dad what he thought I should do, only it wasn't casual at all. It was closer to, "Aaaaaa, what do I do!" After all, that's what he came along for. By this time, I was getting a good look at a boat dock that was starting to fill up the windscreen.

My dad's reply wasn't exactly what I was looking for. He was concentrating, and I could tell he really wanted to help, but he was starting to realize that he might have underestimated the usefulness of a second set of controls. He seemed disappointed in himself when he replied, "I don't know. I really need to be sitting over there." He acted as if he completely overlooked the fact that I might make a mistake and need help recovering.

It was obvious to me that in about six more oscillations, I was going to be sitting up on the dock, so I quit jockeying the power and manipulating the control wheel and just held the controls back and left the power off. The oscillations quickly got smaller, and when they stopped, I added full power on the right engine to turn and miss the dock.

All my dad said was, "I think that's really all you can do in a situation like that. The most important thing to remember is how you got into the porpoise in the first place and not do that again."

I finally figured out how to avoid the porpoise and how to quickly get out of it if one got started. It took a couple of days before my dad got the FAA to give me my multiengine sea and my commercial check ride required for flying air taxi.

I had filled the tanks before the check ride, and I hadn't used more than forty-five minutes of fuel on the ride. I estimated the flight to Dillingham to be two hours and fifteen minutes. The Widgeon held about three hours and thirty minutes of fuel. Thirty minutes of fuel is required for reserve by law, so my dad and I agreed that the Widgeon should have enough gas to make it to Dillingham.

I had a good teacher when it came to skimping on gas. I should have learned not to skimp when it came to gas, but I was paying for the gas for this flight, and after everything I had been paying for lately, I was looking forward to money flowing in the other direction for a change. The gas was cheaper in Anchorage, but the company had gas in Dillingham, so all I had to do was get there.

The next day, I loaded the airplane full of groceries and headed through Lake Clark Pass to start my new adventure. Lake Clark Pass is the pass my dad spent a few days in waiting to be rescued. It was a beautiful day, and I may have been a bit distracted flying over bears, moose, and caribou. I wasn't exactly flying in a straight line, but eventually I found myself about twelve miles away from Dillingham. I was flying at three hundred feet, and I was just starting to think about climbing up to pattern altitude and making a radio call to announce my position when I ran out of gas in my right tank.

I had enough gas in the left tank to complete the trip, but I mismanaged my fuel system and found myself trying to land on a small lake I just happened to be flying over. The fuel management system isn't complicated, but at three hundred feet off the ground, looking out the window at caribou when the engine quit, all I did was reach up and turn the cross feeds on. The procedure is to turn off the empty tank before turning on the cross feed; that way, the engine that is out of gas can now feed from the other side of the plane that has gas.

When I turned on the cross feed, the left engine quit because now it could suck air from the right tank. By now, I was concentrating on landing on the small lake, and I couldn't do anything about the mistake I made. The engines were getting enough gas for a surge of power, but at different times, so the airplane was lunging back and forth until I struck the berm at the end of the lake. The engines were helping me make it to the lake despite the surge, so I had elected to let them surge. Now that I was safely on the water, I jerked the throttles off, and both engines quit.

I had damaged the left float when I hit the berm on the edge of the lake, and now that I was in the middle of the lake, the left wing was no longer supported by the pontoon and was slowly filling with water. I slithered out the pilot window, climbed on top of the airplane, and rushed out to the tip of the right wing to counterbalance the wing with the damaged float. There was a slight wind, and it didn't take me long to drift ashore. I jumped over to the tundra and pulled the Widgeon up as high as I could. I got back aboard the aircraft to use the radio to call an airplane that was flying over. I told them of my predicament and ask them to call my uncle.

My uncle orchestrated a rescue airplane that came out and landed on the lake. He brought with him a mechanic, and I showed him all the damage. We got on the rescue plane and flew on into Dillingham, where we could get parts necessary to fix the airplane the following day. That rescue mission went as planned, and by the next evening we had the airplane back in the hangar. Not exactly the way I wanted to start the season, but it could have been worse. Once we repaired the Widgeon, the FAA came down and gave me another evaluation ride so I could prove that I could operate the fuel system correctly and that I wouldn't make a mistake like this again.

I was doing a pretty good job staying out of porpoises until I landed behind the Grumman Goose. I did not realize that the Goose kicked up a large wave when it landed. I got into the wave and immediately got into such a violent porpoise that pulling the power and control wheel back wouldn't have been enough. I can't explain exactly how I got out of a porpoise of this magnitude without damaging the tail section or ripping off the nose—which history tells us are real dangers in this situation. What I do recall is that it involved the control wheel going from stop to stop a lot, like I had witnessed years ago while I was being rescued at sea in the Widgeon, only I had to add some serious throttle-jockeying to the routine.

I flew the Widgeon for two summers before we hired a pilot for the Widgeon and purchased another Goose. I flew the Goose for twelve summers before my dad and I sold Fresh Water Adventures. My dad retired, and I got a full-time job flying a DC-6. Joe never left my side through all of it.

After forty years and over thirty-five thousand hours of flying in Alaska, I could tell you hundreds more stories just like these. I can't say that Bristol Bay has been completely tamed, but it is a much safer environment now than it was. Most of the larger villages have weather reporting stations, some have weather cameras, and some of your more popular mountain passes even have camera stations. The one thing you can't teach or replace with regulation, however, is common sense.

Flying in Alaska is still a dangerous job, but thanks to the new generation of pilots who have emerged with new fresh ideas, and the new technology that has made its way to the bush, guardian angels like Joe don't have to work quite as hard to keep their assigned pilot from ending up a statistic rather than a hero. Joe's job is much easier now that I don't do the stupid things I used to.

Some people may argue that surviving hundreds of near-death experiences can be attributed to luck. I'm not trying to say that all my stories are going to end this way. Someday, God may decide to call me home. That story will have a completely different ending.

For now, I am blest with stories that all seem to have a familiar theme to them.

My most recent story ended exactly as I have grown accustomed to them ending. I was flying a DC-6 early one morning to Dillingham of all places. The weather in Dillingham was marginal when I departed Anchorage, and when we got there, it was even worse. We attempted two approaches before giving up and heading for our alternate destination. Shortly after we missed the approach for the second time, our number four engine suddenly burst into flames. History tells us that the DC-6 wing will only stay on for six minutes after an engine fire starts.

The DC-6 has two banks of fire-suppressant gas that must be discharged one bank at a time. We discharged our first bank, and the fire went out momentarily but then returned. At this point, a large bowl of good weather suddenly surrounded us. We could see the ground for the first time in over two hours, and we were over a large area of tundra that I was confident I could make an emergency landing on if it came to that. We were approximately two minutes into our fire at this point. Statistically, we had four minutes left to either get the fire extinguished or get on the ground. Is it luck that we went from two options to three options in as many minutes?

The second bank of fire-suppressant gas put the fire out, and this time it didn't return. The third option that had conveniently shown up had given us peace of mind to help us keep our wits about us and fight the fire as a team. I believe the relaxed feeling we got from the bowl of good weather contributed to the favorable outcome. Once we knew the fire wasn't going to return, we left the safety of our little bowl of good weather that God had provided for us and continued to our alternate destination.

In my opinion, God is the only one who can give you this peace—an extra lifeline, if you will. If nothing else, He will just let you know you're not out of options and you were never alone. The third option obviously would have presented its own set of challenges, but there is no doubt in my mind that with Joe at my side, I would have faced the challenges with confidence.

The guys I fly with who know my background will catch me flying outside the box now and then. They will wait until I'm back in the box, and then they'll say, "Did you get your fix?" I'll just smile. Sometimes I wonder if I achieved my goal of being a bush pilot. Then I think, *Who cares?* I go to work, I do my job, and I come home safe. Besides, I think Joe deserves a break.

The End

ABOUT THE AUTHOR

Raised in Bush Alaska the author is a second-generation Bush pilot with over 40 years of flying in the backcountry of Alaska and over 25 summers commercial fishing the infamous Bristol Bay.

CPSIA information can be obtained
at www.ICGtesting.com
Printed in the USA
LVOW10s0957150518

577244LV00001B/2/P